Life and Death in a Single Breath

Life and Death in a Single Breath

Poetry, Musings and Photographs

RM Ullrich

Copyright © 2016 by RM Ullrich.

Library of Congress Control Number:		2016906339
ISBN:	Hardcover	978-1-5144-8629-0
	Softcover	978-1-5144-8628-3
	eBook	978-1-5144-8582-8

All rights reserved. No part of this book may be reproduced or transmitted in any form or by any means, electronic or mechanical, including photocopying, recording, or by any information storage and retrieval system, without permission in writing from the copyright owner.

Any people depicted in stock imagery provided by Thinkstock are models, and such images are being used for illustrative purposes only.
Certain stock imagery © Thinkstock.

Print information available on the last page

Rev. date: 04/19/2016

To order additional copies of this book, contact:
Xlibris
1-888-795-4274
www.Xlibris.com
Orders@Xlibris.com
738356

Contents

Darkest Night 1
Endless Waves 3
Adrift Upon the Sea 5
Unforgiving Truth 8
Today 11
Fear 12
Tomorrow 13
Gentle Touch 15
Treason 17
Becoming Again 19
Rage 24
A Father's Son 26
Life's Journey 28
Moving on – Seasons of change 30
No One Believed… 34
Trust 36
Not Today 38
Life and Death in a Single Breath 40
Minute by Minute 42
Turn Around 45
One More Day… 47
Eternity 49
A Place in the Sun 51
Breathe for You 52
Thrice into the fire 53
Never Ending Song 55

Reflections	57
Tears	59
Love Found and Love Lost	61
Breathless	64
The Release	66
More	67
The Anger Within	69
Love and Light	71
Sleepless Nights	73
A Simple Request	75
Forever	76
Gentle Rain	78
Leaving	80
Between the Lines	82
If	84
Lone Survivor	86
Always	87
Passion's Lady	89
Dark Day Coming	91
Love Me	93
Think of Me	95
Empty Road	97
Long Enough	99
Comprehension	102
Random Thoughts	103
Life	105
Never Ending Hope	107
Thoughts on Relationships	109
Heart's Desire	112
Unfinished Thoughts	114
Faces in the Crowd	116
Believe	118
Love	119

The Reason of the Rhyme	120
Thoughts of a Random Nature	121
Memos from the Chaos	122
This Day	124
Soon…	126
Whispers in the Shadows	128
Waiting on Tomorrow	130
Judgment Day	131
Hallowed Ground	133
Brotherly Love	135
Judgment Falls	137
The Damage Done	138
If you Please	140
Middle of the Night	142
Towers in the Sky	144
The Innocents	146
The Twilight Years of Life	148
Meeting Mom	150
Darkness Falls	151
Stolen Words	152
Yesteryears	154
Words	156
Faded Memories	158
Hi, My Name is Robert Ullrich.	160
Sunday Morning	163
Dust to Dust	166
Gone; but not forgotten	168
Will of Iron	169
Whispered Memories	171
Laura	173
Dolphins Dance	175
Shattered Dreams	177
Reckless Love	179

A Scorpio's Goodbye 181
Vestiges 183
The Lady of the Lake... 185
Truth is Truth 188
Before My Time 190
For Billie 192
Contentment... 194
El Gusto es Mio 196
Home.. 197
Memories, Observations and Lessons learned from a year in Montana (and the journey there and back again)............................ 198
Through the Tears 201
One..203

This work is dedicated to my wife Kim
Without her love and support
I would be forever incomplete.
My life for her love.
Always

Dedications

I would like to acknowledge the following people, living and dead that have had a positive influence in publishing my poetry for others to share.

My mother, Jeri Ullrich (May she rest in peace)
I promised her that someday I would publish my poetry; someday has arrived.

I am grateful to my daughter Jessica, who has pestered me for years to do something with my writing. Perhaps in some way publishing this may someday mend the broken bridge between us.

There are two people in particular that I wish to acknowledge, not so much for inspiration as far as writing or publishing, but rather for helping me come to accept myself as I am. It was not an easy task for either, particularly since I was operating under a diagnosis that I had early onset Alzheimer's. First, thanks to the persistence of Dr. Thomas Chodosh, he has given me back my memories and all but eliminated my anxiety and depression, not by treating me for Alzheimer's, although he did for a season, but for continuing to find another reason for the symptoms that I presented. He is not only my primary care physician; he has become my coach in life as it were. I am truly indebted to Dr. Chodosh for not just treating me, but for caring about me as a person. (Go Vols!)

Second on that list, and by no means does that indicate lesser importance in my life is Dr. Pat Hudson, my psychologist. Yes, I see a psychologist, monthly at the minimum. Deal with it. I went to Dr. Hudson at the recommendation of Dr. Chodosh. It was not an easy call to make. I simply did not want to do it. I can honestly say that I was desperate enough at the time that I literally said to my wife, "Might as well go see her, I sure as hell can't get any worse." I had no expectations, check that, I had negative expectations based on my previous contact with a psychologist who is literally a self-absorbed nut-job; and that is being kind. Fortunately for me, I put that behind me and went to see Dr. Hudson. Dr. Pat has become a refuge for me in this world where I can let my guard down and be who I am, good, bad or indifferent without judgment. The publishing of my poetry is due to no small part on her behalf. I am truly grateful and fortunate to have her in my life, if only for an hour or two a week.

There are many who have encouraged me, and I can't list them all. I will give a special acknowledgement to my friend Mary Kathryn (she with no last name) and to Mike Moyers, whose wife is suffering from early onset Alzheimer's and has been confined to a special care facility for several years now.

I would also like to acknowledge a woman I greatly admired who was loving referred to as "The Lady Ahzmandia" (May she rest in peace), and her husband Diamond. The both were taken from this world by violence in 2008 before they had a chance to meet Kim. I have written about them in my section "Gone, but Not Forgotten".

And last, but far from least; the publishing team at Xlibris that supported me in this endeavor with their encouragement and professionalism, and the personal attention I received that helped my confidence. Even though I have written for over 3 decades, I have never published anything in my own name. Let's be honest here, I don't particularly like negative criticism, and I know that I will get some. Some of the things I have written may offend others, which is something I am not concerned with. If someone chooses to take offense at my words, that is their choice, not my doing.

Thank you for purchasing my book. It is my first and I truly hope that somewhere within the pages you will find something that touches you; moves you or inspires you, and if nothing else I would settle for a smile on your face.

Robert

Personal Reflections

I have been told many times over the course of my life that I was too sensitive, or that I "over-reacted" too often. In context, it was generally intended to indicate I wasn't somehow manly or masculine enough. It seemed that for some reason the depths of my emotional responses, my philosophical ways and my love of writing and the arts, etc. were indicative of a lack of control or strength.

As I traveled through life, at least for a decade or so, I became rather adept at repressing much of my personality through the use of drugs and alcohol. That season came to an end when I entered the road to recovery in 1992, and I began to reclaim not only myself, but my life as well. I vowed when I got clean and sober that I would learn who I truly was, and embrace it. It took years for me to accomplish this, and sometimes the price was high. Regardless, I will never again apologize for a shed tear, a tender thought, an emotional response to a given situation or for reacting passionately to anything or anyone, and I haven't now for many a year. Am I perfect now? Definitely not. Do I sometimes struggle with it? Absolutely yes. Will I ever be satisfied with who I see myself as? It would appear that is also probably never going to happen. It is the principle that changed me; enabling me to come to terms with my troubled past and both positive and negative character traits. The good Doctor Pat Hudson, my psychologist, has been invaluable in helping me to accept that who I am is not defined by what I may or may not have done in my past.

I enjoy many things this world has to offer, and I am rather passionate about some of them. I take as much pride in my poetry as I do in my marksmanship, though I believe I am a better shot than a poet. I am not afraid to embrace my emotions, or lack there-of as the case may be. Thanks to the one I refer to as the Lady Ahzmandia, I was able to offer solace to two young ladies from Chicago that suffered physical and emotional abuse beyond what many of you would be able to comprehend or believe.

Sensitive men aren't weak. Men who have been blinded by their own egos, deceiving themselves into believing that they are strong because they are dispassionate are the weak. They are pathetic caricatures of what a man was meant to be by the Creator. They mistake kindness for weakness and possessions for wealth. They turn their backs on the poor and suffering, all the while professing to be followers of God. One thing I have never been able to reconcile within me is that I have nothing but contempt for man like that; I doubt that will ever change; particularly when it comes to men who abuse their wives and seek to control their lives as though she was a possession.

I would love to blame my drug and alcohol abuse on someone, or something, but I never have and I never will. I did what I did with a free will. I took responsibility for my own actions and behaviors after I entered recovery. I have embraced my character traits, whether perceived as good or bad by others. I have done emotional and physical harm to others, both intentionally and unintentionally. I have violated the laws of society without remorse and helped to obtain justice for those that the system failed. I have made may an amend for my past actions, and yet I am still estranged from my children. I cannot undo what is done. The past is the past and there is no way to truly repair the damage done. Only time will tell if those relationships can be salvaged.

I lost years of my life, squandered if you will attempting to be someone I wasn't. That will never happen again. I am who I have always been. I am who I was meant to be. I will be who I am long after I have forgotten who I was. I am loved by enough people in my life that I feel no compulsion for others to know or accept me. It is the desire of my heart to never again trade the future for the past.; Never again will I accept the judgment of another that I am less than who or what I should be; how they perceive me, how they feel about me or how I choose to express myself or my feelings. I will never again apologize for my passions or my lack of acceptance for others. I feel no need to justify my beliefs, my relationship with my Creator or nature. I am through explaining my past or my feelings about anything or everything that touches my life simply because someone chooses to take offense with me. I can't, for there may very well come a day when I will forget the events and experiences of life that made me who I am, and than perhaps, I will truly understand the meaning of regret.

Darkest Night
March 19th, 1984

The darkness of my nights is relentless
Like a fog it surrounds me
Bearing down upon my soul crushing me
My heart grows weary under its burden
As my life is pressed from me
By the weight of my despair

In desperation I reach out my hand
Searching for a light, searching for hope
Searching for a life itself in the midst of my suffering
The burden of my sins, my failures…
It is a weight that no man can bear
In time, it will surely destroy me

Where is the love of my Fathers?
The love that carried them so far
My heart cries out its need for compassion
For the understanding that it craves
The need the share my life
Is the driving force within

Hope…
Where is the hope that I once knew?
Why has He hidden His face from me?
I am dying as surely as the man in my dreams?
I saw myself cut off from his love by my pride
I watched my life as it flowed from my veins

In desperation I reach out my hand
Searching for light; searching for hope
Searching for life in the midst of my suffering
The burden of my sins, my failures…
It is a weight no man can bear alone
In time, it will surely destroy me

ENDLESS WAVES
October 10, 2011

My mind wanders
Back in time
To another world
And another life
Filled with strife
Memories half forgotten
Of deeds left undone
Promises left unfulfilled
Tarnished by pride
When fear slept at my side
Waves of guilt
Washed over me
Rolling me back
Crushing me down
Without a sound
Darkness found me
Pulled me deep inside
Became my loving bride
Blocking out the sun
Nowhere to turn to
Nowhere to run
Nothing could be done
But close my eyes
And slip into the abyss
One last kiss
Before the dance of death
Would take me down
Cool welcome ground
Burying me in silence
Ending the violence

Sitting by the shore
In darkness no more
Wave after wave
Rolling up on me
Washing my sins away
Soothing my soul
Making me whole
Cleansing my past
Set free at last
By the love of one
That knows the story
In all it's terrible glory
And loves me still
Through the fears
Through the tears
Through the years
Time enough to last
'Til one more day has past

~Robert U~ PS2K ~ October 10, 2011.

It is true what they say; you cannot escape your past. No matter how much you change, no matter how hard you try, it will hunt you down and find you, even if you aren't even the same person anymore. I'm grateful that I don't have to run any more, and that I don't have to stand and face it alone. "My life, for her love, always"

Adrift Upon the Sea

An aimless mist glides across the water
Long rolling swells rocking me, consoling me
Another sleepless night adrift upon the sea
Waiting for the god of the winds to breathe

The sun rises in the crystal clear sky
No clouds to be seen; no promise of wind
Thirteen times the sun has crested the horizon
Since last I moved upon the sea

I close my eyes and see her standing there
Backlit by the rising sun; searching for me
Reaching out to me with her heart
Her love for me leaves no room for doubt

The sun slips slowly back into the sea
Another night surrounds me
A nighttime filled with silence
Save the beating of my heart

Orion looks down upon me
The Hunter of the celestial forest
I can feel my life force fading
As the moon fades into the sea

She knew I was never going to return
Perhaps even before I realized it
Still she watched me sail away
Smile upon her lips; tears upon her face

The sun rises and sets on my last day
A full moon glides through the night
Lighting my way one last time
I know her love watches over me

Long ago I entrusted my heart to her
My secrets; my thoughts; my very being
I knew that if I was ever to forgive myself
It would be through the eyes of another

That is the gift given unto me
A blessing undeserved; unearned
One to make me whole again
A refuge unique in every way

The time has come to me at last
My journey drawing to an end
No regrets haunt my soul
No remorse for deeds done or undone

Orion seems to nod his assent
Polaris watching from the north
Antares is calling me home
A lone albatross glides through the moonlight

Each breath becomes more labored
My heart slowing within
It is time to say goodbye
With no one to say it to

Then I felt her presence
My love had found me upon the waters
Wrapping my spirit in hers
Wringing tears from my dying eyes

She whispers, "I have been
Watching over you for days
As you drifted aimlessly upon the deep
Making peace with nature and self

> "I knew you would not return,
> Nor would I live without you
> 21 suns have come and gone
> Since I left this world behind"
>
> Her smile brushes my lips
> As she reaches for my soul
> Drawing me to her side
> As I close my eyes forever

If I were to attempt to write a thousand poems to be used as my death song, I don't think I will find one more fitting than this. I will never understand the effect of the sea any more than the effect of her love for me. I will argue neither and simply surrender to both.

January 2, 2016

"When it comes your time to die, be not like those whose hearts are filled with fear of death, so that when their time comes they weep and pray for a little more time to live their lives over again in a different way. Sing your death song and die like a hero going home."

Chief Tecumseh – Shawnee Nation
March 1768 – October 5, 1813

Unforgiving Truth
March 5, 2011

It seems I can't remember
No, not any longer
The days before the pain
Perhaps if I were stronger…
It's not pain of the soul
Nor pain of the heart
For they are filled with happiness
Having been given a new start
This is pain of the flesh
Wearing me down
Day after endless day
Night after endless night
Truth shared with only the one
She knows the reason
The length of the season
The toll of this burden
That weighs heavily upon me
I have prayed for just one day
To walk in blissful silence
Free of the endless violence
That ravages my flesh
Challenging my courage
Tearing at my hope
Leaving me spent
Longing for the release
That would bring me peace
Just one day
That is all I pray
Just one day
Free from the pain
Sweet, sweet release

I long for it
I have prayed for it
Never expecting an answer
Never having complained
'Til just this once
This one time I will cry aloud
Having always been too proud
And I will curse the day I learned
That my defenses had turned
And begun to wage war upon me
Unexpected news
Unforgiving truth
Delivered with aplomb

Certainty of death
Though all death is certain
For we are all born to die
Some graciously
Some quickly
And some slowly like me
I have never cursed my God
Nor shall I as I write
So I thank Him for this day
This day unexpected
Filled with happiness undeserved
I cannot curse Him for that
So I will live with the pain
And try to shoulder the truth
That weighs heavily upon my love

~

I will be silent now
Of the why and the how
No one needs the reason
It is in my life but another season

So I will simply pray
Pray for one more day…
One more day than my love
That is my desire
That I shall live
But one more day than her

~

March 5, 2011 ~ simply because there are days that the truth is more than I can bear alone and the pain becomes a white light in the center of my consciousness. I have lived with this affliction more than 8 years longer than was expected, which is over 3000 "one more days". Having put this into words, I will now quietly ask forgiveness of my Creator for yielding to the anger and the fear. There is nothing more I have to say on this matter. I have my support group and I have my wife. My love knows, and bears it with me. She tells me I am enough for her. She tells me that when my body fails me, her love won't. I count on that, every day.

Today

A reminder of how close to death the one that became my wife was on September 14th, 2001.

> The sun rose this morning rather slowly
> Leaving me feeling somewhat lowly
> Until she spoke my name
> Now nothing is the same
> Knowing not what will come of this
> Love and life and her gentle kiss
> No promise of the morrow
> No guarantee against pain or sorrow
> I know this and know it well
> A story of love I am here to tell
> Dancing on the morning dew
> Filled with laughter through and through
> Bringing light into my world
> Around my heart she lays now curled
> Holding on to dreams
> However far off they may seem
> Wanting only to live in peace
> Upon our love forever feast

One day or a thousand years from now it will be no different than it is today. The love you found is yours to keep. None can take it from you. Death himself is but a respite til once again I find my way back to you. Embrace that truth and rest in the knowledge that you are mine.

FEAR

Restlessness wraps me in her arms
Uncertainty draws me closer
Indecisiveness whispers in my ear
"How does it feel to taste the fear?"

Not really sure how I got here
Where the shadows are closing in
Crushing me with their weight
Not knowing when it will begin
For I opened the door again
And now I must pay the price
Shivers running up my spine
Never thought about it twice
Some believe the fear will break me
My world to be destroyed
Nothing could be farther from true
It's only pain I cannot avoid
Embracing darkness welcomes me
Closing my eyes waiting for the sun
Death holds no power over me
Dying means new life begins

Restlessness wraps you in her arms
Uncertainty will draw you closer
Indecisiveness will whisper in your ear
"How does it feel to taste the fear?"

Tomorrow

Time has a way of slipping by me unseen
I looked around and saw it was tomorrow
Not really sure how I got here at all
But I do know one thing with certainty
It is my tomorrow, and I am not alone in it
My past becomes clearer with each passing day
Though the memories there-of become fainter
Moments that were not my finest
Are thankfully fading into the mist of time
Selective memory is an acquired talent
Acquired out of necessity it would seem
Departed loved ones become more saintly
Past offenders become even more despicable
Achievements, once ever so inconsequential
Rise above the savanna like Kilimanjaro
The future…however…stays wrapped in a mist
Nothing getting clearer
Nothing looking nearer
The forks in the path no easier to choose from
Fears of failure still dance in the shadows
Lessons unlearned from days already lived
Time still slipping by me unseen
As I look around and realize it is tomorrow again
Not at all sure how I came to be here
But knowing with increasing certainty
This is MY tomorrow…and I am not alone in it

November 15, 2009 ~ simply because I woke up this morning and realized that time was no longer my enemy. It doesn't matter if tomorrow ever arrives. It isn't promised to me. I don't fear death, not mine at least. I haven't for a very long time. Looking back, I can see the moment when death lost his grip on me. Looking forward, I can see death standing in the shadows, patiently waiting for me to arrive. He is smiling now. He is holding a place for two. Death is nothing to be afraid of, any more than the unknown of tomorrow. Both will get here in time no matter what I do. It's good to not travel alone.

GENTLE TOUCH

Sweetest whispers in the night
Gentle touch that feels so right
Calms my spirit and soothes my soul
Gentle touch that makes me whole

~

So many years I wandered alone
Convinced I carried a heart of stone
Letting the world wash over me
Never imagining I could be free

~

Told to never surrender my heart
Taught to always stand apart
Never give them a chance to know
How deep within your river flows

~

Sweetest whispers in the night
Gentle touch that feels so right
Calms my spirit and soothes my soul
Gentle touch that makes me whole

~

When the pressure of life seems too much
All I need is her gentle touch
When darkness closes in on me
Her gentle touch sets me free

Standing alone in the fading light
Waiting to see that beautiful sight
Watching her from up so high
I can almost hear my spirit sigh

Sweetest whispers in the night
Gentle touch that feels so right
Calms my spirit and soothes my soul
Gentle touch that makes me whole

TREASON

I want to think clearer
Choose to feel better
Some say I could
If only I would
Even I think I should
But how do I change
When it's already changing
Of its own volition
To a new condition
An untenable position
Where I don't know the reason
As to why such a treason
By my mind once so able
To remain quite steadfast
And ever so stable
Keeping my feet on the ground
My emotions in check
All my fears abated
Easily demonstrated
As I slipped through life
With minimal strife
When it came to matters of the mind
Were that it were physical
An affliction of the flesh communicable
Then there would be a solution
To the mental redistribution
Belaying the treason
Giving me a reason

That would end my frustration
With a clear demonstration
That I really would be able
To change the way I feel
Simply by putting my mind to it…
Though that is not the case
There is no such place
That will ever be possible again

10-14-2012.

Becoming Again

~

I am becoming again
Changing, yet not for the better
Slowly, relentlessly creeping into the darkness

~

I cannot describe what lies behind my eyes
I am becoming loathsome again
Unforgiveable as I am unforgiving

~

Wanting isolation for my desperation
As I did in another life
The life that ended on the 5th of January
In the year of our Lord,
As some would say, 1992

~

Truth is truth; I am so fond of saying
Truth is truth no matter how harsh or glaring
As I find myself staring
Into the darkness beyond the light
Beyond the reach of man or beast
Perhaps beyond the Gods themselves

~

Shall I dance and weave and speak in lies?
When at the center of it all
Lays the essence of my life

~

I can no longer see me
Through the eyes of her love
Lashing out at her in anger
Wielding words like knives
Cutting at her soul
Threatening her with solitude
Because I am angry with myself

~

I rage of the rejection by my children
While raging at the self of my past

~

They see me as I was back then
Years of amends mean nothing to them
Mean nothing to many so it would seem

~

I have begun to understand the to the why
The question I have hated all the days of my life
Never wanting an answer for fear of the truth

~

I am becoming again
Accusing myself of crimes against humanity
Judging myself unfit for this world
Seeing myself as I was
Forgetting the man I became

~

Desperation closes in on me
An old partner, come to call
A familiar feeling long ago laid to rest
Or so I have endeavored to believe;
By an unspent bullet on a dark winter's eve

There is no answer for me to weave
With words of wisdom from within
Truth is truth, whether bitter or sweet

~

I have 5 days to find a reason
To turn the page on another season
And accept the truth I became a different man

~

Remember the changes of my life
Re-created by the embrace of death
The forgiveness of a God I didn't believe in
The love of a woman that I don't deserve

~

I see only the man I am becoming again
My past once again, laid here before me
By the hands of one closest to me
Calling me out, cursing me out
Striving to tear my heart from within me

~

So I sit and so I stare
Into the darkness beyond the light
Seeing remnants of truth in the shadow of lies

~

23 years of amends disregarded
Changes made
Lives rescued
Hearts mended

Harms forgiven
Mistakes corrected
While new mistakes made

~

A life of changes
23 years and 137 days of a life undeserved
Re-created by a misfired bullet
On a cold winter's eve
The 5th of January, 1992

~

I have no answer to the question why
I cannot understand why that night I did not die
I don't deserve the life I am living
When I compare it to the life I tried to end

~

The answer seems destined for me unknown
Perhaps it is better for another to understand
One who remembers me as I became not as how I was

~

I have amend to make tonight
Another wrong to try and right
Another harm to try and heal
Seeking forgiveness for my inability to forgive myself

~

This is what I see behind my eyes
When I close them at night to sort my life
Searching for the man I had become
Trapped in memories of the man I tried to kill.

~

May 22, 2015

Unapologetically written, unapologetically shared. If you are someone who cannot forgive my past, welcome to my world. It is a smaller world today, but I still share it with someone who loves me even though she knows I hate the man I was, the man I am afraid of becoming again.

Rage

~

Forgive me my rage for it's not about you
That much for certain of now is true
You seem to find that hard to believe
That is your arrogance and rests upon you

~

The world revolves not, nor my life around you
That much we know is true except it seems by you
My sorrow is mine and you will learn that in time
It has nothing to do with what you think is true

~

Forget my rage and turn the page
There is no need for you here
What is was might not be remembered
What is of now might soon be forgotten

~

Remembered in love by some if not you
That is my hope, whether false or true
Forgotten by most if perhaps save you
That much I believe of the future true

~

So forgive me while I rage against the coming night
For I am neither wrong nor right, however long the fight
To re-capture the fading memory
Of what is was that gave me reason to dance in the pale moonlight

~

Begun on January 9, 2013
Finished on May 10, 2015

This is for those who were a part of my life when it suited them, and have chosen to turn away from me as I write the final chapters of my life. It was started with one in mind; it was finished with several in hand.

A Father's Son

Silent rages of our father's sons
Railing against an apparition
Bottled rage deep within
Yet overflowing at every turn
Who do we really want to blame?
Who CAN we really blame?
For by all the gods that there may be
Someone must surely take the blame

Was it ever really so simple
Or has time rewritten all the lines
Was he the man we remember now?
Or simply just a man
Even so the pain lingers
It hurts no matter how long the years
Since he passed on into the endless night
Though the memories still remain

All I wanted was his love
Acceptance as my father's son
To hear just once "Job well done"
Or perhaps "I love you as you are"
Such was not my father's way
A man born in a different age
A time when fathers stood apart
Believing it must be so

Knowing this will I forgive him?
Knowing this have I somehow become him?
Will my son be able to forgive me in time?
For being my father's son

For Anthony, my son

Life's Journey

"If and When"

You will never forget that moment in time that "when" becomes an "if" again. Subtle changes are still changes. I am always impressed by our ability to hear what we want to hear. When we hear something we don't want to believe, we can actually modify it to fit our expectations or desires. The phrase "if and when" is an oxymoron to begin with. When my father would say to me as a child that we "might" be going to the baseball game on Saturday, I ran and got my glove. It is a rather simplistic example of what I am trying to express, but it says it rather well I think.

"If" is a matter of "hope" while "when" is more definitive in nature. "When" would indicate a measure of time, giving you the expectation or hope of resolution.

I am amazed by the resiliency of men and women who have extracted hope from the darkest of situations and clung to it with fierce tenacity, even in the face of overwhelming odds and seemingly "hopeless" situations. Ones hopes and dreams can rise and fall on the simple word "if". I am no exception to the rule. When an "if" becomes a "when" we leap ahead in our minds to that designated point in time that we have determined will define the "when". However, should "when" becomes "if" again, it can bring us crashing down in fear as swiftly as it lifted us in hope.

I have been advised, from time to time, that some who read my blog have been able to "read between the lines", so to speak, as to my purpose or meaning. I would tell you what I told them. I don't write between them so don't try to read between them. My blog is, at times, nothing more than me thinking out loud in front of the world. This is one of those times.

I have written that I am blessed with the greatest friends on the earth. I am. I consider myself blessed far beyond what I think I deserve, by the love of the one I referred to here as my "Dragon Lady". It is her love that freed me from the vestiges of my past, giving me the desire to be a better man, a better human being, to become the man I always wanted to be, not the man I settled for. I have written little of her in this medium, primarily out of respect for her privacy, and out of respect for her nature.

I have many "hopes" in life. I have "hopes" that my children will find the same level of love and acceptance I have with her. I have "hope" that those I refer to as "Dragon Princess" will one day soar on high; filled with love and life; freed forever from the chains of human bondage that held them captive. I have "hope" that someday I will dance with the love of my life beneath the stars, binding our lives together as one. I have "hope" that she will find peace in my arms and in my heart. I have "hope" that I be able to show her the depths of my love for the rest of her life. I have "hope" that when all is said and done that she will have found in my heart, her true home.

Until that day comes, if indeed, it ever does come to pass, I will endeavour to prepare my world for her and for her own little Dragon Princess. I am honored and humbled by her love. I am honored and humbled that she may place her heart and her life in my hands; and the life and heart of her daughter as well.

So I hope for that day in your life when "if" becomes "when"; remembering that "when" isn't specific; but rather a moment in time when "hope" will become "reality."

Moving on – Seasons of Change

I have always measured my life in seasons. I don't particularly know the reason for that, but it has always been that way, even from my childhood. I never measured the years, which can be a bit of a problem when putting together a resume or trying to remember how long I've been married…but I digress. I measure my life in seasons; good or bad, short or long…doesn't matter. What does is that I can feel the world moving on again. It's been a very long season this time. So long that I almost forgot what it felt like when the seasons started to change again. (Almost)

The change started about 19 months ago when Kim responded to an email of mine. (That in and of its self should have been a damn clue, but like I said, it's been a long damn season here in Iowa.) That email opened a path of communication that led to re-connecting after about 10 years. The result, as most of you know, culminated in our union this year. Some of my friends thought it was a quick decision, but it wasn't. It was 15 years in the making. I mis-fired once before this, but that is a story for the season that is closing behind me and there it will stay.

One of the odd things about my seasons is that friendships and connections rarely carry over from one season to the next. There have been a few exceptions, but for the most part it's been that way. I wonder sometimes why that has been the case, but in the end it is what it is…the world moves on with or without others around us. It's distanced me from my family at times, and isolated me at others. I am sure to a degree it will happen again as I look forward to the coming season. I do know this much, it won't be like the other transitions. I truly believe that I will not only keep many of the friendships I have cultivated in the past 16 years, but I believe I will reconnect with some from past eras in my life. I have already actually, and it's been a delightful experience so far. I was able to restore some of my family connections and I hope that will not fade with the passing of time. But, then again, that is a two way street. It is not solely incumbent upon me to maintain the relationships.

One thing for certain, my lovely bride is going along this time. She said she didn't want to be the reason I moved because that would uproot me. I smiled when she said that because I have never put down roots in this world. Ever. I have always felt that I was passing through, not quite sure why I didn't fit in, but knowing that I didn't. That has never made me feel less of, or left out either. It's been the impetus for much of my life. It has been the reason for the searching, the seeking and the embracing of life…the search for the "why".

Ahhh…why. That very question why has driven men to create entire religions in an effort to answer it. As for me, I finally understood that as far as my life goes…there is no answer to the question why. Why, at least to me, doesn't matter. Knowing why has never made anything easier, or more difficult for that matter. It has never given me peace of mind or kept me awake at nights. Why doesn't answer any question really, it simply begs another one. I can tell Kim one thing for certain as far is it pertains to being uprooted; my roots are in her now, not in this world or this place in which I currently dwell.

It will have been 17 years, come January 7, 2009 since I boarded that plane in Dallas (much like a thief in the night to be honest) and began my journey back to the beginning, the beginning of the quest for answers.

Like so many others before me, I searched for answers to questions not asked in places where they were never meant to be found; questions that I already knew the answers to; questions where the answer lay within me all along; questions that in the end, didn't matter to begin with. So, in the end, why doesn't matter much, if at all. Live, laugh, love and learn all that you can along the way, and you will find what you didn't even realize you were seeking.

The world moves on from time to time. Whether you call them eras, ages, eons, seasons, times or simply years…the world moves on. So do we; all of us. That is, of course, unless we settle for less. Then we stagnate and die long before our bodies wear out and we breathe our last on this earth.

>
> Listen…
> Can you hear it?
> Look…
> Can't you see it?
> I can…
> You will…
> It's just outside your door
> Watching
> Waiting
> Trying to slip inside
> Aaaah…
> Can't you feel that?
> I can…
> You will…
> The gentle touch of love
> Tapping on your heart
> Dancing in your soul
> Setting free your mind
> Smile now…
> I am…
> You will…if you aren't already
> Take my hand
> Reach out to another
> Touching…
> Feeling…
> Embracing…
> Living…
> I am…
> You will…
> It's your destiny

November 16, 2008 ~ because I woke up dreaming of sandy beaches and dolphins dancing just outside my reach ~

Funny thing is that I wrote that even before I realized just exactly what it was I was feeling in my soul. Sometimes I still have to remind myself to breathe, to listen to the silence in the middle of chaos. This season of my life is drawing to a close…this season of *our* life I should rather say this time. I've never moved on like this; with another…(with my mate no less) in my life and sharing the excitement of the coming spring. Here's to the journey…not the destination. Here's to questions never answered and the answers with no reason. Enjoy life. Enjoy it while it's yours to live. And if by some chance somewhere along the way…someone asks you, "Why are you going there?"…Or "Why are you doing that?" Smile at them and don't try to answer the question. Just invite them along…

December 7, 2008…and I turn another page.

No One Believed...
March 22, 2010

There are pieces missing it seems
Scattered remnants of tattered dreams
Dreams long forgotten
Slipping into my consciousness
Causing distress
Stealing my assurance
More frequent the occurrence
Shaking my foundations
With subtle insinuations
That I am slowly losing my way
My mind joins in the betrayal
Oh that it were so simple
To take that sweet elixir
Rolling back the ravages of time
Restore the recesses of my mind
Strength back in my limbs
When I was a younger man
Alas, such is not my fate
It is of now far too late
To rescind some past command
To take a different stand
One less night on the razor's edge
Turn my back on one foolish pledge
And take back the devil's due
Oh if only that were true
I could gather up the missing pieces that seem
Scattered remnants of broken dreams
Dreams now long forgotten
Dreams of life surreal
When my reality seemed so unreal
That no one believed me anyway...

I do not lament, nor do I regret my choices of days gone by. I lived the life I chose. And those choices led me here to where I am today. Right here; right now; and for that reason alone I would do it all over again. Pay the piper; give the devil his due; dance one more night on the razor's edge…simply to be here today with the one that loves me most.

TRUST

You say you want to trust
To let another touch your heart
Then you say are afraid to try
The truth of the matter is that it's a lie
You aren't afraid to try
And we both know why…
You simply want to know the answer first
That doesn't require trust
A crystal ball perhaps
But not trust
You say you don't want to be hurt
That's for certain
No one does
Save the rarified few who thrive in it
The simple answer is that if you live
You get hurt
And you hurt others
It is inevitable
Unavoidable
Necessary and critical
It forms you
Molds you
Teaches you
Life without pain is no life
The only way to learn to walk
Is to walk
You fall
You get hurt
You get up and walk again
It's a life lesson

You say you want to learn to trust
You already know how
You fell down…
It hurt…
Get up and trust again.
~October 26, 2009

NOT TODAY

Someday this will all make sense
Just not today
Eventually we will look back together
And see the way we came
Footprints in the fabric of time
Marking our journey
Showing us what we already knew
Life and death as one
Joined together in love
Gently clearing the mist from our minds
Giving meaning to it all
Purpose in retrospect
Peace in our hearts
Grateful for each moment of the journey
Good or bad
Happy or sad
Gain or loss
No matter the cost
Then we will see the light of the new day
Given to us in eternity
Then it will all make sense
Just not today

December 31, 2012

There are days that we cannot understand the why, when that is all we want to know.

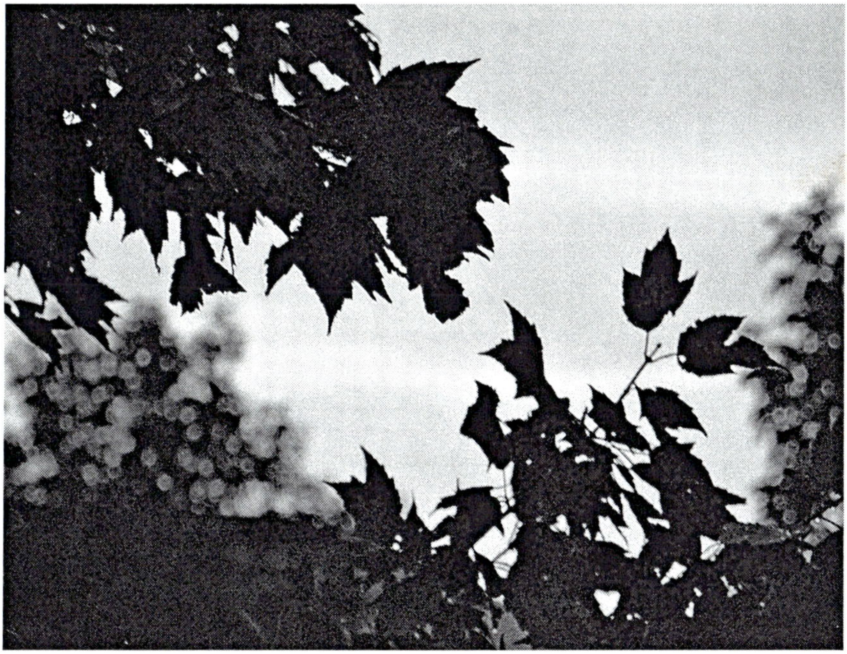

Life and Death in a Single Breath

A lion kills
A gazelle is born
An old man breathes his last
As a child enters the world
An old oak tree struck by lightning
An acorn takes root

Life is but a moment in time
Death is but the same
Every creature born to die
Every life will come to an end

There is no time for remorse
Nor to be wasted on regrets
Today has been given
Yesterday has been taken
Tomorrow is hope on the horizon

A loved one lay dying in my arms
My heart pounding in my chest
Look of trust in her eyes
Breaking my heart
Leaning in face to face
Her eyes closing in death
She breathed out
I breathed in
Capturing her final breath
Life and death in that single moment
The circle of life to remain unbroken
She lives on in every breath I take
Her memories strong within me
Breaking my heart

Life is but a moment in time
Death is but the same
Every creature born to die
Every life will come to an end

You breathe out
I breathe in
The circle of life remains unbroken
Captured in your final moment
Live and Death in a single breath

Minute by Minute

Whispers in the shadows
Fading over the morning mist
It's the sounds of silence that I miss
Leaving nothing to chance
I take your hand
And start to dance
Time grows short while we sway
To the gentle beat of love
While angels watch from above
Drawing out the moments
Day by day
Hour by hour
Minute by minute
Hanging onto each second
There we are together
The storms to weather
Together as one
Time is a thief
She has stolen so much from us
Our time
When the day is done
And you are gone
And then and only then
Will I rail against the selfish gods
To exact my revenge
Justice to be served
No mercy deserved
Long ago I promised her my love
Forever
Always
World without end
But it does end
Time flees before me
Leaving nothing in its wake

Save the scars
And sorrows unimaginable
But it can't take our love away
With the darkness here to stay
While the foolish pray
To keep the demons at bay
Together we dance
Taking a chance
With sweet romance
Knowing at a glance
That time is running out
And yet there is no doubt
With darkness all about
That our paths were meant to cross

With no thought of gain or loss
Never stopping to count the cost
Tis better to have loved and lost…
Some say yes
Others say no
And there are those that cannot
Will not
With no hearts to try
They sit in the shadows and cry
Never tasting the bittersweet tears
When you conquer your fears
No matter how short time is for us
We will always have this dance
Having taken the chance
And made our stance
And tasted sweet romance
For a moment
A moment in time
Time without end
In a world full of darkness
You were my light
When hope had failed

And against the gods I did rail
You touched my soul
And turned my world around
Whispers in the shadows
Fading over the morning mist
It is this sound of silence that I miss
Leaving nothing to chance
I take your hand
And start to dance
Time grows short while we sway
To the gentle beat of love
While the angels watch from above
Drawing out the moments
Day by day
Hour by hour
Minute by minute
Cherishing every second

For anyone who has ever wanted to turn back time.

Turn Around

You wonder sometimes who to trust
When nightmare rumbles turn to dust
Shadows dance across your mind
Searching for any help you find
Dance and sing and scream and shout
Until you drive those demons out
Turn your face to the rising sun
Take what's left and make a run

Turn around and look at me
Someone's got to set you free
We both know you won't last another day
If someone doesn't take your fears away

Sit and listen to your own heart beat
Feel the passion and feel the heat
Is there something truly wrong?

You thought the love was strong
There's nothing more to say or do
I only hope your life's not through
Until it's over you'll have to stay
And listen to what your heart's to say

Turn around and look at me
Someone's got to say you free
You won't last another day
If someone doesn't take your fears away

One More Day…

~

I have seen much in my life…
Things that made me smile
Things that made me sigh
From time to time things have made me cry
For joy or for sorrow…no matter
Tears come unbidden
I have stood upon the mountaintop
I have lain on the bottom of the sea
Wandered in the desert
Swam in the cold mountain waters
I have seen the sun rise and set time and time again
One ran into another…
Til now
All that changed when I held her in my arms
And watched with her eyes
Saw what she saw
Filtered through her love
"One more day" I whispered to her
"One more day is what I want"
"One more sunrise…
"One more sunset…
"One more night with you"
I whispered the same to the sinking sun
Cast my wishes into the sea…
One more day…

~

November 30, 2008

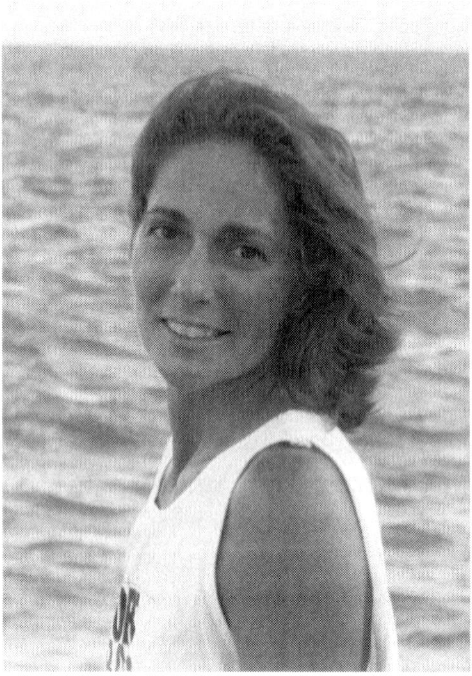

ETERNITY

She stood silently with me
On that barren mountain peak
Leaning into the howling wind
That whistled up through the trees
Chilling us with its bite
The world lay off in the distance
Turning slowly into the future
That was when the earth stood still…
The fierce winds suddenly calmed
The birds fell silent
The trees held their breath…
The seconds stretched out before us
Seconds into minutes
Minutes into hours
Hours into days
Days into years
An eternity of moments captured for us
As "Now" became "Forever"
Forever for me and my love

March 15, 2009, somewhere in the black hills of South Dakota

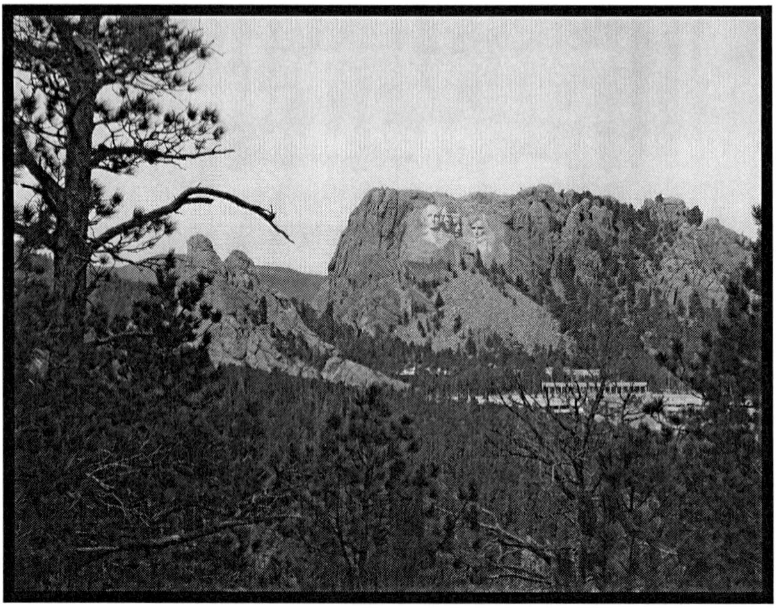

A Place in the Sun

~

Through the tears
Overcoming her fears
Words like spears
Carry the message
To my soul
Touching my heart
Wanting for her
What she desires
One last journey
To the shores of the sea
Giving her what she never had
A place on the earth
To call her own
A place to be free
Of the fears
Shed of the tears
Where her soul
Is at peace within
One with nature
Blessed of God
Giving of her self
Touching my heart
A place she calls home…

~

For my wife, because sometimes I hear what she doesn't say.

Breathe for You

When that day is long and you can't go on
Let me breathe for you
When your heart is aching and your bones are weary
Let me breathe for you
When the burdens you carry weigh you down
Let me breathe for you
When the light fades from the sky and silence falls
Let me breathe for you
When you can't go on and your strength fails
Let me breathe for you
When you reach your journey's end
Let me breathe for you

You gave me hope
You gave me love
You gave me life
You gave me everything

Let me breathe for you

Thrice into the fire

The first time I was spared
The second time I turned away
And others suffered the price to pay
Blinded by my pride
Senses dulled by fears
Days fading into years
Memory of a memory
Shadowed in the light
Two lives liven
One life given
One life taken
Both lives forsaken
Void of hope
Overcome by darkness
Seeking forgiveness unnecessary
Absolution not needed
For sins not committed
Judgments undeserved
Thrice into the fire
Once more required
To cleanse my foolish pride
Of wishing I had died
When a second chance was given
Now the pathway taken
Closes the door on my past
A lesson to be learned
To hope at long last
Forgiveness unnecessary
Absolution never needed
For sins not committed
And judgments undeserved
I am but a man
In spite of myself
Because of my self

In spite of God
Because of God
For if God is God
Then forgiveness is unnecessary
Absolution is unneeded
Sins were never committed
Judgment never passed
Yet, if in the end lies a void
Darkness unavoidable
Dreams unattainable
It is of no concern
To a man with lessons learned

-August 23, 2015-

Never Ending Song

Welcome home my friend
To the song that never ends
I've been singing it for you
While you were working through
Those trials in your life
Seasons full of pain and strife

We struggle to transcend
But it's hard to comprehend
The struggles that we face
When in that darkest place
We find ourselves again
Where we've already been

We lose our place sometimes
Start paying for our crimes
When all we had to do
Is to ourselves to be true
Those that love us know
They've seen the show
Watched us shed our tears
Consumed by our fears
Aware of nothing more
Then lying on the floor
Listing to the sound
Of our world crashing down

Breathe in
Breathe out
You have never been alone
Just pick up the phone
You will find them waiting
Anticipating
Your fears abating

Welcome home my friend
To the song that never ends
They've been singing it for you
Because their love is true

-January 20, 2008-

REFLECTIONS

You chose to that let the bitterness in
Watched it slipping under your skin
Knowing there was no way for you to win
All the while your defenses wearing thin
When all you had to do was smile
And it might have left you in little while
Maybe traveled along for another mile
Touched you in a much different style

You gave resentment power over you
Don't try to deny what you know is true
You're the one that tried to break on through
To change the reflections of another's view

I gave you chances to make it right
You had the choice to stand and fight
Now it's come down to this
Age-old saga with a modern twist
There's nothing left for me to say
You keep waiting for yesterday
It's lost forever in the faded past
While the future rushes by so fast

There is no starting over again
No way to change life's refrain
I was given but one life to share
Of that truth now I am fully aware

There is but one path I've taken
And my past I've never forsaken
I carry it with me each and every day
Never forgetting the tears of yesterday

~

~ October 31, 2008 ~

Tears

A child wept today
Tears of sorrow
Long held captive by her fears
Unable to shed them 'til now
A child wept today
Tears of regret
Burning against my skin
Long held captive in her heart
A child wept today
Tears of loss
For years lost
That should have been hers
A child wept today
Tears of release
Needing forgiveness
For sins never committed
Struggling for peace
Seeking the meaning
Where there is none to be found
A child wept today
Tears for her father
For all those years lost
At such a horrific cost
The prices paid
For the memories made

~~~~~~~~~~~~~~

She wept today
While I held her close
No way to ease her pain
Only time may find a way
To heal the damage done
By the mother of this child

And mend the scars upon her soul
Once again perhaps to be whole
Free from the guilt that almost took her life
Guilt that was never hers

For my wife, that mourns the loss of the man that raised her as his own flesh and blood. She was able to spend the last 7 months of his life with him in Montana, but at a price that nearly drove her to give up on life. It is written somewhere that we are to forgive as we would be forgiven. Perhaps that is true, but not for me, not for the damage done to her spirit. I will never forgive, nor forget the damage done to her by the one that was supposed to love her most. If that means that I will not be forgiven, I can live and die with that.

Love Found and Love Lost

Much has been written of romantic love, brotherly love, erotic love, love of friends, of God and of nature, to name a few. Hell; much is written of the love of alcohol and drugs for that matter. I cannot, nor will I attempt to define love, simply because I don't think it can be defined.

Truthfully, I am not even sure love is an emotion, at least not for me. I have told many women over the years that I loved them. I am on my fourth (and by all the gods there may be) final marriage. Much of what has inspired me as far as my attempts to capture the concept of love to me; has been the love and acceptance I found in Kim. I do know, after three marriages that ended in divorce, however love may be defined, it isn't enough of and by itself to sustain a relationship. I have also discovered that to be true when it comes to my children and our struggles to re-connect after I spent about 20 years absent from their lives.

I have spent the last two years or so meeting as often as my insurance would allow, and even after they stopped paying for it, spending an hour or two a month with Dr. Pat Hudson, who has become not only my psychologist, but a wonderful source of advice and encouragement. I mentioned her in my acknowledgements, but that doesn't do justice to the impact she has had on me. In short, she has given me the knowledge and tools to accept myself as I am, regardless of the opinion or judgments of others, including my family and children.

I wanted so very much to believe that I wasn't the same man I was in the 80's and early 90's, when my life was driven by selfishness, greed, avarice and good dose of drugs and alcohol. However, the truth is quite simple. I am still that same man. I have the same character traits and dispositions I had then, and I am fully capable of returning to that same style of life. The difference is I have learned to not act as impulsively and, to a degree at least, I have learned to value the consequences of my actions; not on myself, but on those that love me.

The reason I shared that is because I was anything BUT impulsive when it came to my wife, Kim. There was an instant and palatable attraction between us the day we met on that elevator at the old Conway Inn in Waterloo, Iowa. An attraction that was difficult for me to resist, too, but I did. We spent a lot of time together because of my job and hers over the next 4-5 years before falling out of touch.

It was April of 2007 when Kim emailed me to see how I was doing. I will never forget the morning I walked into PIPAC in Cedar Falls and she came out from behind the receptionist desk to hug me. As impulsive as it may seem, though it wasn't, I decided then and there that I would spend the rest of my days in this life on earth and forever in the next with her.

Our life together began on November 11, 2007 when she moved in with me in North Liberty. She quickly became not just a part of my life, but a part of me in a way I never expected. Do I love her? I believe that by any definition of the word you can find, yes I do. I want her to be all she ever wanted or dreamed of being. I want her to be free of the guilt that was laid upon her as well as the memories of the abuse she suffered mentally and emotionally. I do not need to "fix" her. I love and accept her as she is. My only desire is to provide a safe and fertile haven where she is free from judgment, and free from her past. That includes people from her past, even family members if necessary; and I have taken measures to insulate her from them.

My friend, Diamond (gone but not forgotten) once said to me "Shit Spike, peoples are always talkin' shit about how they would lay down their life for someone they love, but then they treat 'em like they were nothing to them. The real measure of love ain't whether or not you are willing to die for someone; it's whether or not you would kill for the ones you love. Dying is easy, living with blood on your hands ain't, but if that is what you have to do to keep your lady safe, you best be prepared to pull that trigger".

Those were not empty words to D. He backed them up in July of 2008 when he went to Juarez to avenge the murder of his wife.

I have asked myself that question before, "Would you kill for Kim?" The only way to truly know is if I am ever put in a situation that would require it of me. I believe that I would, and when I ponder the possibilities and the ramifications, it causes me no anxiety when I consider it.

Truth is truth.

BREATHLESS

The first cut isn't the deepest
The first cut only begs for more
Savor it when your flesh craves another
Passion's call touches your soul
Leaving you breathless
Out of control
Craving more
Begging for release

~

The first cut takes time
Nothing worth doing is done quickly
Sorrow's kiss upon your lips
Tearing at your heart
Draining your strength
Fading into the darkness
Lost in the silence

~

The pain touches your soul
Bringing you back
Closer to the light
Closer to love
Closer to the beginning

~

They say the first cut is the deepest
But it's the last that carries you
Holds you
Caresses you
Leaving you breathless
Out of control
Craving more

Begging for release

~

The steel blade cuts the flesh
Love cuts deeper
Slicing to your core
No escaping the pain
Believing love is the answer
Understanding love is the reason
Knowing love is the blade that cuts
Holding you close
Leaving you breathless
Out of control
Craving one more cut
Begging for release

The first cut isn't the deepest
It's the one you will remember
You will surrender to the flesh
Embrace it
Be consumed by it
There is nothing else in this world
Worthy of love

~

Savor it always
The first time I cut your flesh
Leaving you breathless
Out of control
Craving only more
Begging for release

~

That first cut
That bonded your flesh to mine
And stole your heart away

The Release

He watches her quietly from the shadows
She is entwined in his heart like none other
In a way only few could ever understand

How she has grown with passing years
The little girl stands a woman before him now
His weathered cheeks streaked with tears

Remembering back to the day he found her
A lost and wandering soul; steeped in fear
Cloaked in shadows; yet a glimmer of hope even then

She gave herself to him believing it for a lifetime
Surrendering her identity to become one with him
Never knowing a day like this would come

He knew in his heart that it would not last forever
For that was not meant to be; not for her
His role in her life was not to keep her; but to set her free

Her eyes slowly widen with understanding
As he opens this final door for her
Revealing the truth he had hidden from her until now

Overcome with sorrow, yet filled anew with hope
She sees a new future unfolding before her
Seeing with new eyes, her tears join his as they flow

He had chosen to make the ultimate sacrifice for her
Trading his happiness for her freedom
Releasing the joy of his heart to soar on high with the Eagle

MORE

it is all that I have
all that I can give
would that I had more
more of life
more of love
more to give
if it was sooner
than later
there would be perhaps
more of me to share
more life
more love
more
it is too late for that
for remorse
for regrets
for second chances
let alone third
it is all that I had
all that I could give
and give it I did
without a thought
without regret
without remorse
freely gotten
freely given
freely taken

without a second thought
let alone a third
on that
you have my word
my life
my love
all that I had to give

The Anger Within

I never meant to make you cry
No matter now the reason why
It falls upon me the harder to try
To see the anger within me die
You aren't the cause
Nor ever the reasons
They are my character flaws
My own personal treasons
I never meant to bring you tears
Unleashing selfishly your lingering fears
Memories recalled from darker years
When words were only used as spears
Piercing you through the heart
Bringing you to your knees
Words meant but to tear apart
Never your pain to ease
You are never the cause
Nor ever the reason
My character flaws
My own personal treasons
You make my life worth living
With your love forgiving
Never my past reliving
Nary a moment of misgiving
There is no way to redo the past
Gone for now but never at last
Tainting a future unsurpassed
Unless my love stands in contrast

I never meant to make you cry
No matter now the reason why
For your love I will forever try
To see the anger within me die.

~

because sometimes…an apology simply isn't enough

LOVE AND LIGHT

~

I woke up this morning to another day
It doesn't matter
It shouldn't matter
What the darkness has to say
Light and love will always stay
Where they are cherished
Where they are nourished
Darkness cannot overcome the light
Unless I give it a place in my life
If I listen to her words
Giving darkness the right
And I yield my happiness to the night

~

I woke up this morning to a better day
It really does matter
It really should matter
Who I listen to and what I say
Light and love will always stay
Where they are welcomed
Where they are wanted
I have no one to blame
If I lose sight of the light
And listen to the shadows of the night
Giving her a place in my life
Where she steals the joy from my heart

~

I woke up this morning to her love
That's what really matters
That's all that should matter

I woke up this morning and saw the light
Lying by my side
Filling me with happiness
Whispering her words to my soul
Giving me strength to face the day
Driving the darkness back for the moment
Keeping the shadows at bay
Her words drown out the whispers of the night
For one more day, in this world all is right

November 27, 2012

I wrote this is for my wife Kim on the occasion of our 4th anniversary. There isn't much I can do to celebrate it with her this year as we have in years past. As much as I would love to take her for a walk on the beach as we did 4 years ago when we exchanged our vows, I will settle for a stroll by the river, or a walk in the park, hand in hand with the one that loves me most. I tell her often, "My life, for your love", and that is the truth of it. Her love gives my life meaning, making every day worth living, and every day that I had lived worthwhile. In her, I found peace with my past and hope for my future. Now, as the future fades from me, it is today that I must cherish with her, and find my moments where I can. No one can take that from me. No one has the right to. No one can take her from me, save the God of my understanding who will hold her for me until I find my way back home again to her side. For if God be God, then I have nothing to worry about for He will understand. If He doesn't, then He isn't God after all. No matter, for I have experienced a lifetime's worth of happiness and love in the 5 years we have been together. She taught me the true meaning of light and love, and captured it for me in a simple gift of beads and string so that I am always reminded of it. I don't know how one is supposed to repay a gift of that nature other than to cherish it and hold it close to your heart, which I do every day.

My life, for her love, always.
To one more day

Sleepless Nights

Restless day after restless day
Waiting
Wondering
Wanting
Time slipping into timelessness
Day slipping into night after endless night
Moonless nights
Silent nights
Filled with echoes of unspoken words
Waiting to be born
Sleepless nights
Restless day after restless day
Waiting
Wondering
Counting the moments

Time slipping out of timelessness
Sliver of light on the horizon
Faintest of hopes takes flight
Time shall pass in time
Precious moments captured in an instant
Held in her love
Forever

~ September 5, 2010 ~ for Kim on the day of
her return from 3 weeks in Montana ~

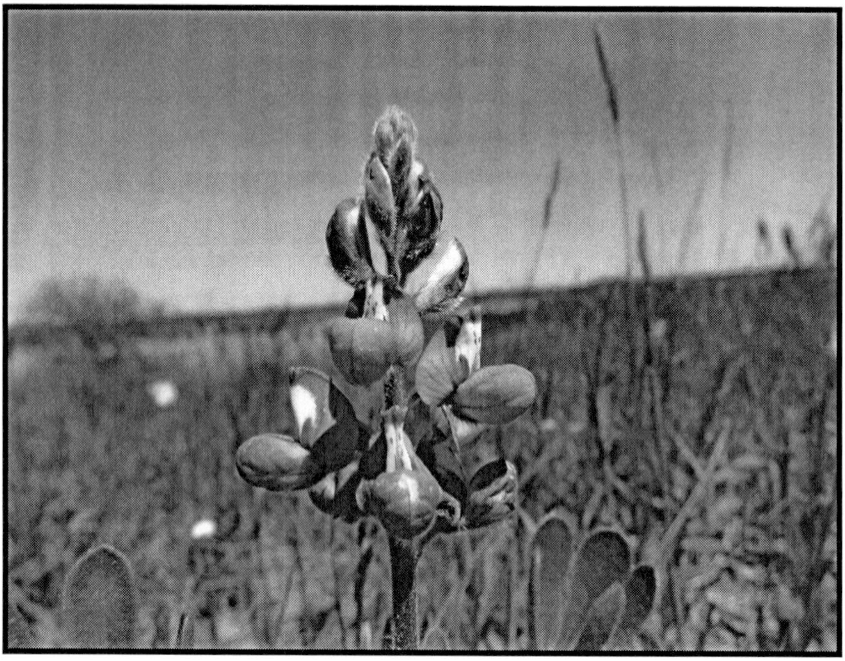

A Simple Request

She grinned at me somewhat sheepishly
Then whispered just a little breathlessly
"I would like another *'wow'* if you please"
And gave my leg just a little squeeze
Lying where recently she had flung me
I pondered her request quite diligently
"Why yes I can do that wow for you,
If you would release my leg for a minute or two"

Seems I had lost my place for a moment
Last I had known I was awaiting the torrent
Not really sure what happened next
But I do know for sure that it was pure reflex
Lord only knows what she was expecting
But I will bet the damn farm there'll be no regretting
The moment that dragon finally took flight
And sent me flying…ass end, over appetite…

FOREVER

You know you love him
You always have
You always will
That is why it hurts
Always doesn't exist
Forever is a myth
You love someone you cannot touch
You desire someone you can never have
So your heart grows weary
With every breath you take
Every step you take
Waiting for him
Wishing he was there
Praying to a god with no ears
Pleading with a god of no heart
You knew it from the start
And it tears your world apart
Watching it slip away
He will not stay
No matter if he says he loves you
No matter if he says he cares
The world moves on ever turning
The memories to never fade

There is no need of forgiveness
No harm was done
No blood was let
It is quite easy to forget
That this isn't forever
A least not yet

You believe you loved him
You thought you always did
You think you always will
That is why there is such pain
Always doesn't exist
Forever is but a myth

Gentle Rain

Gentle rain falling
Whippoorwills calling
Flowers blooms abounding
Listen for the sound
Of angels on the wing
And all the love they bring

When I close my eyes forever
Will everything remain the same?
Whe I close my eyes forever
Will anything still remain?
When I close my eyes forever
Will it take away the pain?

Nothing is as it seems
Holding on to fading dreams
Listening for the muffled screams
Children wrestling with their fears
Watching the shadows drawing near
Cheeks glistening with lonely tears

Hold your breath
Hide from death
Close your eyes
Nothing dies
Take my hand
Make the stand

Gentle rains of spring
Robins on the wing
Hope of the morrow to bring
A smile lights your eyes
Time begins to fly

Open your heart to me
I will set your spirit free
Listen to my gentle plea
There is no shame
Your spirit is clean
You seek the freedom due
To one as willing as you

Leaving

I see it in your eyes
Filling me with lies
No matter what you say
I am never going to stay
You had your chance
I may have tried back then
Then you hid your heart from me
Claiming you needed to be free
Laughing at my tears
Preying on my fears
Believing I didn't know
The seeds of discord sown
You took my love for granted
All I ever wanted
Was to see you smile again
Knowing that you were whole
I found you broken
Lost and dying
You wanted something from me
Turning on your charms
Until I took you in my arms
Believing in your lie
That you only wanted to learn to fly
Like an eagle on the wing
I wanted only your love
And I would have carried you up above
There's nothing I wouldn't have done
If you had been a righteous love
Time showed me I had gone astray
And the price that I would pay
To find my way back onto my path
And deal with destiny's waiting wrath
For I had turned my back upon my quest
Settling again for something less

That was then; This is now
I found my way back somehow
Back to the place where she would be
Waiting patiently for us to be free
Through this life I had wandered
Many an opportunity squandered
Lessons hard
Painfully learned
Within my heart I did yearn
For her fiery presence
To taste at last the essence
Of life meant to be
When from my past I would be free

Between the Lines

There's a reason I never mentioned your name
Though I will love you just the same
It wasn't me that turned this inside out
Sowing discord and seeds of doubt
Lesson learned yet again
That to speak one's mind might be a crime
It wasn't me that took offense
Putting forth a needless defense
One last time I will tell you this
Please try your best to understand
There is nothing written between the lines
There never was
I'm a writer
At least that's what some would say
Sometimes my words are callous and bold
Taking inspiration from many things
Sometimes in the night my words take flight
Weaving a web of verbiage vague
A flow of words that can be a plague
And someone takes offense
Requesting of me to make a defense
A defense I cannot sustain
For it would cause others pain
So here is my reaction
Don't let it be a distraction
Remember that I loved you
While I gently close the door

Perhaps I can never be truly clear
If you are reading between the lines
When there is nothing to be found
Let there be peace between you and me
If by chance our paths should cross
Know that in my heart you are remembered
When a shiver of lonesome runs through me

IF

If I close my eyes
I can feel your touch
If I close my eyes
I can taste your kiss
If I close my eyes
I don't miss you as much
If I close my eyes
I can believe this true
If I close my eyes
I can smell your hair
If I close my eyes
The sun stands still
If I close my eyes
You are standing there
If I close my eyes
The world bends to my will

There is nothing more to say
Then perhaps a prayer to pray
That in the morning light
This love that feels so right
Will carry us through the fight
And you will never fade from my sight
Come with me and stay
Never to walk away
Place your hand in mine
Travel with me to the end of time

If I close my eyes
The eagle flies
If I close my eyes
Nothing dies
If I close my eyes
It's you I see
If I close my eyes
Forever here with me

Lone Survivor

Restless days, sleepless nights
Bodies thrash together
Tensions rising into the sky
Wrestling with the fire between
Love
Hate
Peace
Fear
Driving us to the limit
No retreat, no surrender
There will be but one survivor
Will on will
Steel on steel
Sparks flying from my anger
Words thrown like daggers
Piercing her to the heart
Shattered love
Broken dreams
Never will I admit my wrong
Though blood was let, still no regret
I can't see past my folly
Crushing her love to my chest
Destroying it in my anger
I can't let go
I must let go
Or all she is will perish

~

Restless days, sleepless nights
Walking the streets alone
Wrestling with the fire
No retreat
No surrender
I am the lone survivor

Always

Tears of sorrow
Tears of remorse
Wondering at the source
There is no way to rejoice
Knowing that you bleed
Torn between the two
Seeing the pain in you
Watching the shadows grow
Love dying ever so slow
Though it is not love that dies
But rather the hope thereof
Like a fleeting moment
Lost forever in the mist
Never having kissed
Longing for release
Searching ever for peace
That love is supposed to fill
Your fears to be stilled
Yet your world shatters
Dreams left in tatters
Wanting to rejoice
Wondering at the source
Wanting to be above it all
While feeling ever so small
There is no other way
If love is going to stay
It must be this time
Any less would be a crime
Take my hand
With me you can stand
Fears released
Forever in peace

You by my side
No need to turn and hide
This love will never die
Loving you
The perfect thing to do
Seasons will change
And our love will remain
Always

Passion's Lady

~

Hope that lingered lost in time
Forever would have been the crime
Watching from afar
Waiting for the chance
To embrace sweet romance
Join him in the dance
And wish upon a star

~

Wanting nothing more
Then just her heart to pour
Fearlessly at his feet
Listening for to his voice
Afraid to make the choice
Yet daring to rejoice
In love never so sweet

~

I've always kept my eyes on you
Waiting for the moment true
Watching from afar
Waiting for the chance
To embrace this sweet romance
And join you in the dance
While reaching for a star

~

Passion's lady came to me
Wanting only to be free
Moving while she had the will
To make a new start

Strengthened with a lion's heart
Weary of being always apart
Wanting to be cherished still

~

Take my hand and come with me
Let me set your spirit free
Filling you with desire
Trusting me with your love
My precious mourning dove
Filled with fire from above
And I will take you higher

~

Hope that lingered lost in time
Forever would have been the crime
Watching from afar
Waiting for the chance
To embrace this sweet romance
Join together in life's dance
And catch a falling star

Dark Day Coming

Dark day coming, heading my way
Night upon the horizon, blackness destined to stay
Holding my breath, reaching for her
Just beyond my reach, drifting in the mist
Motionless, tears in her eyes
Begging me, begging me not to cry
Begging me not to die, begging me to live
I cannot reach her, I cannot feel her touch
Just the pain, feeling nothing but her pain
Feeling her drained, felling her deepening sorrow

~

Dark day coming, heading my way
Night upon the horizon, blackness destined to stay

~

God how I love her, God who doesn't hear
God who doesn't care, God who wants her more
Taking her from me, taking her from us
Selfish fuck that He is, taking her away
Nothing left for me to do, but wait upon the end
Death moving slowly
Draining her, draining me
Draining the life the one I love
They say it is better to have loved and lost
Then to never have loved at all
Better for whom?

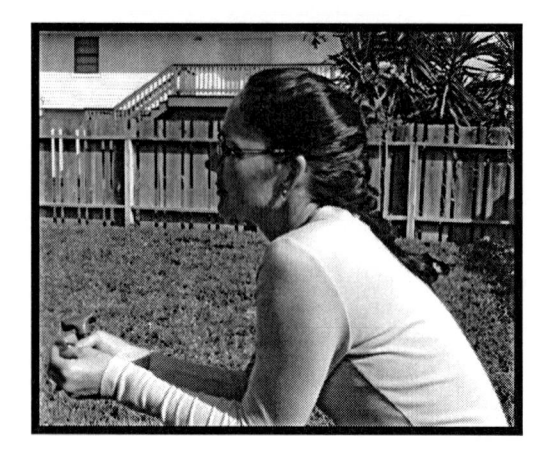

I faced the darkest trial of my life during the year we spent in Montana. I made the most difficult decision I have ever had to make. I chose to let Kim go if that was what she truly needed to do. She stood on the edge of the abyss, drained of hope by the constant beating down of her spirit by one that claims to love her, all the while attacking her spirit; ungrateful, unappreciative, blinded by her own selfishness, using her, debasing her, threatening her, denigrating me, so filled with bitterness that it was a cancer that was eating Kim's spirit. Then came that fateful night when Kim didn't believe she could live with it any longer. She was doing everything she could, including swallowing her pride and fighting for acceptance. She could have died that night at her own hand. I told her that I loved her, and that I would not stop her. I also told her I would avenge her death in no uncertain terms if it came to pass. I spent the night sitting in the dark, waiting for the sound of death. In the morning she came to me and told me that because I was willing to let her die, she would live for me. I will never forget that night, nor will I ever forgive the one that drove her to that precipice. Truth is truth.

LOVE ME

Nothing's as it seemed to be
After she turned her fire on me
I have to let her love me
She can set my spirit free
Listening to the sound of her voice
Removes from me a choice
Drawing me to her fire
Filling me with desire

~

Life flows from her soul
Healing my heart, making it whole
Nothing seen can compare
To the beauty of her standing there
Lighting flashing in the skies
Fire dancing in her eyes
Heat of passion burning my skin
Opening her heart and pulling me in

~

I feel the time passing by
Unaware of reasons why
Mists of memories fade to gray
No need to turn away
Savoring the vision of her standing there
Watching over me, my heart laid bare
No more need to hide my tears
No more shame to be found in my fears

~

Nothing is as it seemed before
I opened my soul in search of more
She is going to love me now

All my defenses torn down somehow
Turned my world upside down
Bringing me home with the sound
Her voice whispering low
"Take my love and just let go"

THINK OF ME

Feel that shiver running up your spine?
You're going to feel it again
Every time you think of me
And how you used to be so free
Back when your heart belonged to me
And when you cry yourself to sleep at night
Remembering how it felt so right
Knowing all you ever had to do
Was give me your love and keep it true

Feel that shiver running down your back?
Watch the sky as it fades to black
Every time you think of me
And how you used to feel so free
When you heart belonged to me
There's nothing left for you to try
There's no more tears left for you cry
I gave you everything I had to give
I gave you every reason to live

Feel that shiver running through your soul?
It's knowing that in your heart is now a hole
Every time you think of me
And how you used to be so free
When that heart belonged to me
I would have done it all for you
If only you had loved me true
My life I would have given for you
But you simply couldn't see it through

So feel that shiver running up your spine
I want you to feel it every time
Every time you think of me
And how you used to feel so free
Back when your heart belonged to me
So when the darkness closes in
And you feel the shadows on your skin
When your blood runs cold in the middle of the night
Think of me, and remember when…

Empty Road

Cold wind cuts me like a knife
Empty road stretching out before me
On my own again, alone in life
Feeling the crush of the coming night

All she wanted was to be free
Free to be all I told her she would
She loved me hard and loved me sweet
Trusting more than I thought she could

She stumbled once and nearly fell
Reaching out so I could bring her back
Eyes searching mine for forgiveness
All she saw was cold and black

She was young and wild and full of life
To her it was a simple mistake
Though she trusted me with her heart
She choked back tears as I tore it apart

She paid the price for my selfish pride
As she knelt in silence before me
Knowing she had let me down
Was more than she could let me see

So here I am on my own again
While that empty road fills my sight
Cold wind of regret cutting like a knife
Feeling the crush of the coming night

Where of where is she tonight?
That sweet young vision in white
You trusted me with your heart
Then wept for us when I tore it apart
Forever left to sit and wonder
At the deadly cost of just one night

Long Enough

I sit here while you sleep…
Keeping watch over you
Your breast rises and falls as you slumber
I can see your pulse in your neck…
Your eyes flutter as you dream
A smile dances across your lips
A sigh escapes your soul…

It seems as though I am dreaming
Dreaming of a life I never knew
A life I never planned
My past sometimes haunts me
From time to time it nudges me
Reminders of decisions made
Paths taken
Hearts and lives left in my wake
Still…no regrets
Every step I took brought me closer
Closer to that moment in time
That moment when I first laid eyes on you
And you took my breath away

I breathe a little easier as you sleep
It's quiet here now
Nothing but the sound of my own heart
To keep me company as I watch
It's hard not to look to the future
It's harder to let go of the past
Reminders of decisions made

Paths taken
Hearts and lives left in my wake
Still…no regrets

I have seen the sun rise and set in your eyes
Held you close as darkness fell
Felt your touch in the deepest recesses of my soul
Freeing me
I have lived a lifetime in your love
A love I never deserved
A love that cleansed me of my past
Remnants of decisions made
Paths taken
Hearts and lives shattered in my wake
Now…no regrets

Breathe in…
Breathe out…
Feel the warmth upon your skin
Feel the peace deep in your soul

I never wanted to live forever
I only wanted to live long enough…
Long enough to hear the question
Long enough to find the answer
Long enough to know the reason why
Long enough to feel the passion
Long enough to make amends
Long enough to dance with the dragon
Long enough to soar with the eagle
Long enough to dance with demons in the warm firelight
Long enough to sing with angels on high
Long enough to learn the meaning of life
Long enough to learn the meaning of death
Long enough to laugh

Long enough to cry
Long enough to love

~

Thanks to you…I finally have.
If it all ends tomorrow
If I never see the light of another day
With you at my side
I can truly say that I have lived life
Not watched
Not wandered through pointlessly
But lived it
Never an innocent bystander
I won't pretend to be when judgment falls on me
I meant to do it.
I don't regret it.
I'd do it all again…for one more day with you.

~

December 20, 2008

Comprehension

Holding my breath
Dancing with death
Feeling her touch
Never too much
Searching for release
Looking to the east
Listening for her voice
Making the final choice
Dream's daughter smiling
Closing the miles
Opening my eyes
On wings of hope she flies
Ever closer to my heart
Knowing it from the start
Holding out her hand
Making her final stand
Rising like a dove
My life for her love

Random Thoughts

I look around me and see it's time to travel. It must be, the trees are all dressed up in their finest colors. I can feel it in the wind, can't you? Even the caterpillars are starting to drag out the wooly sweaters, heading across the roads for warmer climes…

I moved back up north for this. For this changing of the colors, the seasons, the moods…

Last fall changed everything as far as the seasons go. I brought my dragon lady home to me last November 11th. With her came her daughter Jackie that I have come to love as my own. They accept me as I am. My past an open book to them. All that I did, good or bad, right or wrong…

I was molded by those experiences into the person, the man I am today. I am comfortable in my own skin at last. For years I searched for meaning and truth in this world of ours; testing the waters, if you will, of many ways of living, and many ways of life. I have stood before the faithful and preached a message of hope from a man called Jesus. The hypocrisy of so-called men of God drove me from their midst. I needed compassion and love more then any other time in my life. They turned their backs on me in my hour of desperation and set me adrift without remorse.

I have danced with the devil, as some would say, in the darkest recesses of the human experience. Not watching and waiting, but actively embracing the darkness to extract whatever I could from its suffocating grip. The family of man I formed in the midst of the shadows never turned their backs on me, not even when I walked away and closed the door behind me.

It has been a very long road: filled with all manner of life along the journey that brought me back to where it all began. Not the beginning of my life, but the quest for knowledge. The answer was with me all along in the changing of the leaves…

Seasons come, seasons go…friends come, friends go…the world moves on in times of joy and in times of sorrow…love dances like a leaf in the highest branches of the trees waiting for the wind to set it free…in the darkest moments of your life, spring is on the horizon…waiting to renew the world, and your soul all over again. Winter can be cold and bitter where I have chosen to live; which makes spring that much more wonderful to behold as the leaves return…year after year without fail.

Someday spring will not return for me, or for you. When that day comes, it isn't me that will suffer, but those that are left behind. Some will be angry, some will weep long into the night…some will dance for joy because they knew me and knew my heart…and I dare say a few will simple be glad I'm dead…no matter, the end is still the same.

Live, laugh and love like there was no tomorrow, simply because there is no promise you will live to see another day. If you are going to hate someone, or something, do it for what they did to you, not for some perceived offense upon another. I've been guilty of that, taking up offenses from time to time…I will most likely, contrary to my own thoughts here, do it again.

There are many things in this world that make me smile, many things that make me laugh. There are things that touch my heart and bring tears to my eyes, tears of happiness, tears of sorrow and sometimes… tears of compassion.

The one I call my dragon lady, my babygirl, my lover, my companion, my pride, my joy, my desire, my wife and above all my mate…brings them all to my eyes. No one has ever done that before in my world, or in my life. She has made the journey worthwhile.

Seasons come, and seasons go…she won't.

~ October 26, 2008 ~

LIFE

Bad things happen to good people
Somehow that's supposed to change the way you feel
If you are in the middle of something you can't understand
Try as you may; unable to comprehend what is happening in your life
Filled with measures of conflict and strife

Good things happen to bad people
That doesn't make it right that you still have to fight
Trying to understand why not those who deserve better
All the while wicked men prosper
While the wise profess to understand deeper

It is incumbent upon me to change the way I feel
This is the charge laid upon me
That I reach down into my soul and
overcome the fear of the unknown
Charged to do battle with my mind
To find a way to win while there is still the time

Forgive me since I don't agree
With those that say I should be able to change the way I feel
That I take note of the suffering of others in this life
All matter of challenges, sickness and strife
And simply change the way I feel

Bad things happen to good people
That doesn't change the way I feel in the middle
of something I can't comprehend
Try as I might, they will never understand
what is happening to my mind
Stripping me of both space and time

Forgive my anger and my frustration
Or forgive it not as it is only directed at me
If I perchance fail this day to overcome the
darkness and fear in my mind
It does not mean I have forgotten the suffering of others
I simply cannot remember my own life

Never Ending Hope

Images flash in the darkness
Voices in the shadows
Unseen hands pulling you back
Wrapping you in solitude

You can hear their whispers
You can almost see them
As you slowly slip into the mist
Dancing on the edge of consciousness

What is it that you seek?
What was it that you lost?
How can there be such fear in you?
When you are loved so much

Whispers in the wind
Sadness in your soul
Hope of things to come
As life collects its toll

Time keeps passing by
Soon to pass without you
Leaving the wind to whisper
Never ending like your love

If I had the power to turn back time
I wouldn't change a thing
Everyone that I have been loved by
Gives my heart cause to sing

The world moves on
The heart will begin to feel again
Pain removed by memories of love and laughter
And I will hear your voice among those in the shadows

Never ending whispers in the wind
Never ending sadness of the soul
Never ending hope of things to come

One beginning
One day
One night
One heart
One soul
One kiss
One touch
One love
One life
One death

Never ending promises of love

Thoughts on Relationships

I have always done some of my best thinking while working with my hands. Today I hung sun shades on the front porch and repaired a bamboo wind chime. I also came to understand something about relationships, negative relationships that is.

Throughout my life I have made friends from school, work and social settings from all walks of life. Professionals, business leaders, workers of white and blue collars, clerics and clericals, law enforcement and military and saints and sinners as they say. Some of my friends have MBA's and doctorates; others GED's and criminal records. Having a doctorate versus a criminal record doesn't make a difference to me. I try to judge people on the content of their character, not the sheepskin or lack thereof on a wall. Two of my closest friends were a psychologist and a convicted murderer. They also happened to be man and wife. They also happen to have both died in 2008.

Some of the above were and still are a positive influence in my life, living or dead. I think of something every day that my father, or mother, or one of my grandparents or teachers, former bosses or life-friends said to me that had an effect on my character and life.

I have also had the misfortune of developing negative relationships in life. Some of those negative relationships ended with positive results, and are cataloged in my memories as lessons learned. Others simply proved themselves a waste of time.

Over the years I have sometimes tried to change a negative relationship to a positive one through amends of one sort or the other. I have had some successes, and some failures. It turns out that some people simply prefer to carry resentment versus offering forgiveness. I learned one thing about myself, in that I do not require forgiveness. I require that I make amends in my life to change the behavior or attitude needed to address the mistakes of the past. I also learned through the process that sometimes it is far better to leave the past undisturbed.

This brings me to my minor epiphany while hanging sun shades last weekend.

Some relationships are not meant to salvage. Some people are not worth the energy needed to try and co-exist in peace with them. One of the major lessons learned from our year in Montana is that some people simply prefer to be miserable, the consummate martyrs of life, black holes of negative energy that can only find satisfaction by bringing everyone around them down in one way or another. These types of people are like a cancer in your life, and I finally understood that you have to treat them the same way. Some cancers are treatable, and that is what we try at first, just as we do with someone who is, or shall I say should be important in your life, we try and treat it. Sometimes treatment works, and sometimes it doesn't. The point is, we don't ask permission of the cancer to treat it. We do what we need to do to make our lives better and healthier. In the worst case scenario, we cut the cancer from our lives.

That is what I did. Cut the cancerous relationships out of my life. A harsh analogy, perhaps, but I am given to more direct approaches to life these days. I was always quite the mediator in my personal and business lives. It served me well my years working in night clubs as a bouncer (yes, skinny old me was a bouncer and a damn good one). I was damn good because I never started fights, I prevented them. I defused extremely tense situations, including one very intoxicated woman outside Cheers in Fort Worth who pulled a gun on me; but I digress.

I no longer have certain mental filters when it comes to dealing with others, whether it is my supervisor and employees at work; my neighbors or life relationships. Basically, the words fail me and I tend to use the first word I think of, and it is sometimes not as delicate as one would hope. I can rarely finesse my way through a confrontation anymore so I am more apt to take the direct, if somewhat offensive approach. I have at work, and much to my surprise managed to keep my job. I have with my neighbors, and one of them will most likely never talk to me again; I can live with that.

I spent last weekend trying to salvage a relationship that didn't need salvaging. The connection I was trying to repair wasn't worth the energy I was expending, so I cut it off. I didn't even bother trying to leave a door open for a future reconciliation. There is no need. Nothing good could ever come of it, and I don't have the time or inclinations to waste time on negative people. They are cancers in your life and if you can't treat them, cut them out.

June 29, 2014.

Heart's Desire

Perhaps people are just people
No more
No less
Neither good nor evil
Perhaps one moment of kindness
Towards an evil man
Can change the essence of his world
Perhaps redeeming him
Giving him hope
Giving him back his life
I don't know the answer
Perhaps no one does
So I will leave that to the philosophers
Live with honor
Die with grace
Touch someone's heart
Give someone a reason to smile
Give a broken heart hope
Fix a shattered dream
Give someone vision of possibilities
The Lady of Lake said it is the child in me
That makes the broken feel safe
They have no fear of me
I hope that to be true
Nothing would give me more joy
A shrink once told me I have no fear of death
I believe that to be the case
I have never wanted to live forever
I simply want to live long enough

Long enough to see them laugh
Long enough to see them loved
Long enough to see them cherished
Long enough to see them dance
Long enough to see them free

~For Tikee and Chloe~

Unfinished Thoughts

Never ask the reason why
Knowing will only make you cry
You will realize it's far too late
To change the path of pending fate
You're the one that made the choice
And in your folly you did rejoice
Until the tide turned on you
Shocking dreams fading blue

I've never been afraid of dying
Not for lack of trying
It's more a fear of living
In a world most unforgiving
With a cosmic fear of flying

There's something in her eyes
That tells me what I need
There's something in her smile
That shows me who I am
There's something in her touch
That heals my very soul

We celebrated an anniversary May 31st. Not a wedding or birthday, but rather a homecoming. We arrived back in Rockport on a warm Friday afternoon, May 31st 2013 from (as I like to call it) my third and FINAL move to Texas.

The passing of time has softened some of the edges from our year in Montana, others remain razor sharp and I imagine they will always be that way. There were blessings there, and trials; such is life. Acquaintances and memories made and is want with both, some good and some not.

As I lay in bed last night watching Kim sleep, I thanked my God for the journey. Life was never the destination as I have come to understand or Heaven the great reward that some paint it to be. Life is the reward, the gift and the greatest blessing of God, this life. The fact that I get to share the remaining years of it with the one that loves me like she does will remain the greatest mystery to me in this world, never understanding it, never feeling worthy of it, but all the while cherishing every moment of it.

> There is a season for every reason
> So they say
> For us to play while children laugh
> For some to sing of the coming year
> Looking to the east into the rising sun
> Hold your breath; it's just beginning
> Time to soar on high
> Where the eagles fly
> And dare to try to understand the why
> Of words left unspoken
>
> I dreamt my world crumbled
> I faltered and stumbled
> As she came to me in tears
> Succumbing to her fears
> Asking for her release
> Seeking but one more day of peace
> In a world she once knew
> Before the reality came true
> Reality
> My dreams have become real
> Nothing I can't feel
> Memories not mine
> Lost in another time

Faces in the Crowd

Faces in the crowd
Passing without a glance
Your heart beating too loud
You dare not take a chance
Don't look them in the eyes
They'll see you bleeding inside
Your smile the fears belies
Lest they see the pain you hide
A child whispers as you pass
Dare not breathe; don't look back
Your flesh is made of glass
She can see your soul is black
Reaching out she takes your hand
Shocking you to silence
Not knowing why she would try
To make you feel safe and loved
Now you begin to weather the storm
Faces in the crowd
Casting a fearful glance
Afraid they can hear your heart so loud
Dare to take the chance
They cannot see you bleeding inside
They don't know the pain you bear
They only wish they were free
To shed their tears and break their pride
Looking down into her eyes
This child of wonder at your side
No fear of you or what you hide
Knowing she will tell no lies
Your doubts with nowhere left to go

Breathe in
Breathe out
Peace will find you in all due time
Breathe in
Breathe out
There is no need to hide
No fear of death to rob your life
We all have fears and doubts
Everyone faces uncertainty and strife
Failing to live your life would be the only crime

BELIEVE

Let the laughter ring
Let the children sing
Of life and everything
That love can bring
Listen to the flowers grow
Dancing in the wind as the rivers flow
Taking their time; going it slow
Waiting for the coming snow
Little things that make you smile
Get you to walk that extra mile
Come with me for just a while
Life's not supposed to be a trial
Listen to the beat of my heart
Telling you its okay to believe in the art
Of dancing in the dark
With the one that holds you close
The lone that loves you most
And once you've made the choice
You will see the world rejoice
As it joins you in the dance
Of love and sweet romance
Not knowing they too have the chance
To capture love with a single glance

LOVE

Hard as steel
Cold as ice
Burning as the sun
Full of life
Embracing death
Gently held
Freely given
Freely gained
Open handed
Ready to strike
Reaching out
Gathering in
Gentle as a lame
Dangerous as a lion
Building dreams
Tearing down walls
Hard as a diamond
Shatters like glass
None can repair
Eternal
Temporal
Handle carefully
Love
Yours
Mine
Ours

The Reason of the Rhyme

If you had truly cared
You would have shared
Every moment good or bad
Angry, happy or sad
You would have asked
You should have asked
That's all I would need
For us to succeed
A moment of your time
A semblance of caring
For times worth sharing
Not waiting to be told
While the destiny unfolds
As to the reason or the rhyme
I wanted my life to matter
To you as much as anyone
But you never extend your hand
You simply wait on mine
I have no more to give
Only what's left to live
Reasons worth sharing
For those still caring
As to the reason of the rhyme

~September 23, 2012~

Thoughts of a Random Nature

Listen to the wind as it wanders
Weaving its way through the trees
With never so much as a "by your leave"
Or even an ever so polite of a "please"
It carries the song of the mountains free
Winding its way to the shores of the sea

Catch if you can the rays of the Sun
Hold them closely 'til day is done
Let them fill the cockles of your heart
When from your loved ones you are apart
They will keep you safe and warm
Nestled away from strife and harm

Hark unto the herald's song
The joy of the morning won't be long
It slips quite gently through the edge of night
Waiting quite breathless for the coming sight
The timeless beauty of dawn's first light
The sun once more on wings takes flight

~November 13, 2012~

Memos from the Chaos
-April 16, 2007-

In memory of those that lost their lives on the Virginia Tech Campus. I was traveling that day with my elderly mother from Iowa to Houston for my sister-in law's funeral service. I tried to capture the essence and emotions of what those around me were feeling as we watched the story unfold while waiting in various terminals en-route.

A child cries as her mother smiles
Hushed whispers behind me while laughter resounds from in front
A young man kisses his crying love
Friend hugging friend as business men watch in silence
Stunned by the scene unfolding before us
Pseudo intellectuals argue the reason, dissecting
the stream of consciousness
Analyzing the why and the what in heated debates
Never knowing the truth that there is no
reason "why" for what we see
No reason why the slaughter, no reason why for the carnage
One man takes that to the grave with him…
My mother sits in indifference; her dementia
has no way to process this
A young Asian couple sits quietly in tears;
looking at the faces around them
Searching for something; afraid of everything in this moment
They are not to blame; but they feel it pressing down on them
Accusatory stares; glares of anger from the ignorant that abound
A bull of a man weeps openly; a young man sighs in sorrow
I feel a hand on my arm; a whisper in my ear
A young woman not wanting to believe her eyes
Slips to the floor beside me crying in silence
Unable to comprehend the why

I know I am somewhat detached; watching over my mother
Preparing to lay a loved one to rest
In time, it presses into me; taking my heart by force
And I begin to feel
Deep; hard; filled with rage; yet drowning in compassion
Gnawing at my very soul
Wanting to know the reason why
When no reason will ever justify the pain and sorrow
Of those left behind

This Day

Cool breeze drifting across the water
Refreshing the night
Palm trees rustling
Dawn hovers just below the horizon
Waiting for her moment
Sliver of a moon
The only light
Faint whispers on the wind
Speak to me
Remind me
There is but one day
This day
This day that was created for us
Rejoice in it
A great heron's call splits the silence
Nature's guardian of the shores
Reminding me
There is but today
This day that was created for us
Dawn is coming
She kisses the horizon
Black sky edged with purple
Silhouetting the trees
Nudging the birds from their slumber
Speaking to me
Reminding me
There is but today
I shall rejoice in that
It is one more day than I have a right to
One more of thousands more days gifted to me

Dawn has arrived
The night yields gracefully
Reminding me
This is the day that the Lord hath made
I will rejoice
And be glad in it.

October 3, 2010
Robert U. ~ written in real time as the night passed into morning ~ Finished at 6:54 a.m.

Soon…

There's a bite to the wind
As it cuts through the skin
Chilling the soul within
Winter's first dance
Seems harmless at a glance
Lulling the trees into a trance
Stripping them of their leaves
Leaving them naked to the world
Unaware of their shame
They remain the same
Watching over the dying land
Colors fading to brown
Leaves scattered about the ground
Foragers prepare for the coming sleep
Looking for treasures to keep
Against the impending darkness
The sun weakens as winter approaches
Barely able to clear the horizon
The once mighty ruler of the day
Begs for scraps at nighttime's table
Just a touch of kindness
Hiding in the half-light
Wanting only to ease the pain

Of winters deadly grip again
Soon…
Soon enough…
Soon enough indeed…

~

Robert~PS2K~October 30, 2009~on the occasion
of the 56th anniversary of my birth.

Whispers in the Shadows

Hushed whispers in the shadows
Eyes downcast in fear of retribution
Longing for a peaceful resolution
Begging softly for absolution

You don't know what to say
You don't know what to pray
You don't even know if he wants you to stay
Searching desperately for a way out

He broke your heart before
He'll break it again
So you try to refrain
Your life, what little that remains

Emptiness fills your soul
You will never fulfill the desired role
Slipping slowly into a deepening hole
When all you want is to be cherished

Hushed whispers in the shadows
Eyes downcast in fear of retribution
Longing for a peaceful resolution
Begging softly for absolution

Trying desperately to make restitution
For the words you spoke in haste
That laid your world to waste
Leaving you battered and debased

Fear not the coming morrow
Though your heart is filled with sadness
Your mind touched by madness
The nights ever so relentless

Listen for the sound of my voice
Giving you a chance
An opportunity to rejoice
Whispered in the shadows

-April 29, 2007-

Waiting on Tomorrow

Waiting on the moment
Not sure when it will be
But I am sure that it will be
Maybe not today
Though try as I might
It is what I hope for
Maybe not tomorrow
Though that would be nice
Suffice it to say
That nice is a relative thing
Nice relatives are a good thing
So I will get back to waiting now
Waiting on the moment
When then will become now
And when will be no more
Blended into one
The past is my future
My future to melt into the past
Happening so fast
So I go back to waiting
Waiting on the moment
Not sure when it will be
But I am positive that it will be
Definitely not today it seems
Try as I did though
It is what I am hoping for
Maybe tomorrow
If tomorrow remembers to come

~ November 8, 2012

Judgment Day
August 1, 2008

There will always be questions without answers in this life. There will always be stories with no happy ending; and justice that will never be served on many that deserve it. To say that I am angry would be a simple thing, but it goes far beyond that. There is a void in my world, a void that was left by the murder of one of my closest friends, followed closely by the death of her husband who went into Jaurez to exact retribution on those that took her from him. I am angry for the void left in other lives as well. She was no saint; far from it. She had honor, and took care of many who could not take care of themselves. Through her I was able to provide emotional support an encouragement to two young ladies in particular. Tikee and Chloe, whose last names are unnecessary; her loss from their lives will be far more devastating that it could ever be in mine.

I miss them dearly, all of them. Together they taught me to laugh at myself; to let down my guard around someone that by all intents in purposes could have easily killed me if it became necessary. They showed me the strength in kindness; they stirred my soul; challenged my beliefs; protected those I sent to them from a world that had taken everything but their lives. They gave me a new perspective on the meaning of honor; even though they were called thugs by the world at large. They treated me with respect even before I earned it, and they loved those that I held dear to my heart simply because I did.

There is a darkness that dances deep within my soul. I have reached down into it from time to time in the course of my life to extract energy that burns like fire as it courses through my consciousness. It is because of what they taught me that I can dance in the darkest recesses of my soul without fear that it will overpower me. That is where I am now as I write these words; embracing the rage and wanting retribution; judgment for those that took them from us; harsh judgment. I won't linger here for long; I can't. In spite of the loss I feel, not only for myself, but for so many others that looked to them for direction and leadership, friends and family alike; I have responsibilities for the one that loves me most. I have many reasons to be grateful in spite of the loss. Death comes to us all so I will not rail against the gods for taking them. God didn't take them; they were taken from this earth by men. None-the-less I have my own to care for and I cannot carry this rage with me without causing her harm.

My life is the sum total of every experience I have had; good or bad; the influences of every person I have met and shared time with; for better or for worse. I will forever be thankful for the time I was given in their lives; the hours on the phone, the thousands of games of scrabble and dominos that I played with Chloe; the consoling and support that Tikee needed in her darkest hour. I will always be grateful to them; the ones I called "The Lady of the Lake" and her "Thundercat" D.

If, or should I say when judgment falls on me, I hope to be able to stand with my head held high and my eyes fixed on the one who will judge me. I cannot speak to right or wrong; sometimes they are impossible to separate in the moment.

There are those walking this earth today that don't deserve to. No one can question that. "Who are you to judge?" you are asking yourself right now, and I have no answer for you. We are told that "Thou Shall Not Kill", yet history has proven that Christians will slaughter entire races in the name of God, just as the Hebrews did in their time; and the radical Muslims are doing today.

You may judge me as you see fit because I will judge anyone that comes into my life; especially if it involves the ones I love. In the meantime, rest assured that in the end; neither your judgments or mine will sway the judgment of the One that sits on High.

Hallowed Ground

You spoke of honor as though you had it
You demanded respect you never earned
Whispered deceptions in the darkest shadows
The time has come to reap what you have sown

~

Rant and rave and scream or cry
Rail at the gods; begging them why
As I drop the hammer on another round
And lay you to waste on hallowed ground

~

Through their lives you callously wandered
No regrets for the love you squandered
Given freely by those who need it most
Covered in blood you offered a toast

~

Beg and plead as you grovel and cry
Rail at the gods and wonder why
As I drop the hammer on another round
And lay you to waste on hallowed ground

~

The story of your death will spread far and wide
Men will tremble and children will hide
They will hear the brutality of how you died
Torn asunder by your ignorant pride

~

Justice will come in the middle of the night
Nowhere to run, no way to fight

You brought to the innocent countless tears
Now they will haunt you with endless fears

~

I'll sit and watch while you bleed out and die
Listening to you rail and beg for your life
Then drop the hammer on one last round
Leaving you to die on hallowed ground

~

August 1, 2008

BROTHERLY LOVE

What more could you want from me?
How much did you think I would take?
It's time for you to make a stand
Time perhaps to be a man
I've truly done too much for you
Gone the extra mile too often
I can't save your life
I can't make everything right for you

So you stand there looking at me
Begging with your eyes to be set free
I didn't put those chains on you
I only told you what was true
You made your choices on your own
Seeing now that time has flown
No way to turn back now
No matter how hard you try

You lived your life with no concern
No regard for lessons to be learned
Laughing at those you left behind
How could you think I wouldn't mind?
You took from others without regard
Proving to them that life is hard
And now you stand there once again
Asking me for more

Your smile will fade as I turn you down
Knowing you never saw it coming
Believing I will come to save you
When I will be coming to make you pay
You squandered the life you were given
There is little need for you to go on living
So now I lay you down to sleep
And pray the Lord your soul to keep

Judgment Falls

Cool wind caresses my soul
Reminding me
Blessings unexpected
Happiness undeserved
The debt I owe
A life for a life
The promise given
Yet I live on
Unfettered by guilt
Strangely so
Time passing
Always passing
Never waiting
Drawing ever closer
To judgment day
No forgiveness there
At least none for me
None required
None given
A life for a life
The promise given
My promise
And I will answer for it
Breathe in
Breathe out
'Til judgment falls

~

February 27, 2011.

The Damage Done

Why do you sit there with your head in your hands?
Making pointless demands
Trying to stave off tomorrow
When I will visit you with sorrow
The likes of which will make men shudder
And whisper prayers to the gods
Prayers of gratitude that they aren't you

The time will come for you to pay
For sins and horrors of yesterday
When you thought you were above it all

Every tear you shed will fall on parched ground
There will be no one to hear your cries
Only the scavengers aloft in the darkening skies
They will feast upon your flesh before the blood dries
No forgiveness for you will be found
As in your fears you slowly drown
Knowing why I've come for you
Remembering the one whose blood I am avenging
As I smile and watch your life slowly fading

Justice will come to you at last
Though you thought that you had made your peace
And escaped the consequences of your past

Time passes slowly when promises are kept
I made a vow to the one that became my wife
A vow I will keep 'til the end of her life

So remember this when you lay there dying
You owe her thanks for all those years you lived
After the damage was done…

September 28, 2009- Remember, sometimes justice is served in silence. And, as my wife just reminded me…"you need to feed both sides of your soul"

If you Please

A warning glance in your direction
Captured by the moon's reflection
Softly whispering in the breeze
"You are standing in my way, if you please"

*

I have come to claim her as mine
Meant for me through endless time

*

I've no real desire to bring you pain
Though I'll not shed a tear just the same
You are standing in the way of the one I desire
Blocking me from her cleansing fire

*

A flicker of a smile touches my lips
Subtle movements in my fingertips
Moving forward while standing still
I'll not hesitate if it comes time to kill

*

Far too long you've held her there
Mocking her daily with your callous stare
Crushing her dreams without a care
Driving her closer to the brink of despair

*

I have come to claim her heart as mine
Meant for me from the dawn of time
I'll not abide your presence much longer
The craving within me only grows stronger

*

Last warning glance in your direction
Captured clearly in the moon's reflection
Whispering by the gods in the breeze
"I've come to take her home, if you please"

*

Let there be no doubt as to my intent
I will take her with me; your time is spent
Walk away with what you have left
And I just might spare you a painful death
October 17, 2007

Middle of the Night

What are you going to do
To try and set things right
When death comes calling
In the middle of the night
No time to bargain
No mercy to be found
You had your chances
Thought it better to deceive

~

Now you stand there
Arms at your side
Throwing out apologies
Trying to make amends
You should know better
You call yourself a man
You should know better
Then to make this unrighteous stand

~

Many are those that trusted you
Turning to you for direction
Waving your hands and blaming God
Was your ultimate deception
The awaits a special kind of hell
For those who made the innocent prey
I will sing a song and dance a jig
As the scorpions tear their flesh away

~

You sit there now with tears in your eyes
Watching your world wither and die
Don't dare ask for sympathy
Seeking forgiveness not to be found
Embrace the end of your life
For you there is no mercy
And I will sing a song and dance a jig
While scorpions tear your flesh away

January 2, 2007

Towers in the Sky

Hold your breath
Hide in the shadows
Don't make a sound
Stifle your beating heart
For death is passing near
He will snatch the life from you
If you look him in the eye
There is nothing for you to fear
Unless you've made a choice
That sets you on his path…
Protect the innocent
Comfort the sick
Shelter the poor
Love thy neighbor
Do unto others as you would have them do unto you
That was His charge
That was His message
Yet you build monuments
Towers of gold, silver, glass and steel
Stretching to the sky
The higher the better to catch the sinner's eye
Modern day Towers of Babel
Worthless now as it was then
Testimonies to the egos of men
Not houses of prayer to your God
Those buildings won't save your soul
Nor will they save you from the coming Death
The more spiritual you claim to be
The more you run from your destiny
Trying to outrun your fate
Not knowing it is far too late
You tell the lost they will be reborn forever
That's the hook that brings them in
Then you speak of God's great love

While you fleece them like so many sheep
Twisting the truth with strands of lies
Threatening them with damnation
Promising them blessings from God above
For 10% of their hard earned funds
The poor struggle to make ends meet
While you build yourselves multi-million dollar homes
Homeless wander without hope in our streets

While millions upon millions are spent to build even larger towers
Modern day Towers of Babylon
As worthless now as it was then

~

So heed my advice and hide in the shadows
Try not to make the slightest of sounds
Stifle if you can your beating heart
Death is coming for you soon
Sent by the God you claim to serve
To end your life and claim your soul
When he looks you in the eyes…

March 7, 2009

The Innocents

Fire and ice have purged her soul
Her pride destroyed and run to ground
Darkest of nights lonely and cold
Whimpers of pain the only sound

Walking in the shadows of others
Eyes downcast for fear of falling
Cold winds of November cut to the quick
Hands like ice freezing to the railings

The darkest night has yet to come
Though she has no way of knowing
Thinking the worst has come and gone
Yet the demon's claws not yet revealed

If she could see what I see
She'd know she was already free
If she could see what I can see
She would everything ever dreamed to be

Someone will have to answer for her pain
Justice will find him in all due time
Retribution will embrace him
He will tremble in fear like a little child

Woe unto those that harm the innocents
May the gods have mercy on their souls
For I will surely not shed a tear
When death comes calling to collect his tolls

Blessed are those that protect the innocents
Sheltering them from the evil of the night
Giving them love and hope abounding
Trying by all the gods to treat them right

January 8, 1987

THE TWILIGHT YEARS OF LIFE

I turned 62 last October. I don't feel it; for the most part that is. There is no doubt whatsoever that my body feels it; however my heart and mind have yet to come to a consensus on the subject.

I labored for almost 5 years under the belief that I had contracted early onset dementia. I based that on the well educated and professional opinions of a psychologist, an M.D. and a reputable Neurologist. It has been hard for me to share this with my friends and family; primarily because I was accused of "over-reacting" by some, and given the deepest compassion and support by others. I feel like I somehow deceived them. A young man by the name of Wayne Burger has been waling for a cure for Alzheimer's in my name for several years now. I know that it will not disappoint most to find that it was not the case, but rather a case of misdiagnosis. I cannot harbor any ill will towards the medical professionals that treated me during those 5 years. The medications they prescribed and the psychological assistance I received all had a positive effect in reducing my symptoms. Regardless; it was Dr. Chodosh who found an answer for my symptoms through trial and error. Thanks to him, my quality of life has improved dramatically, and the clouds in my mind have dissipated to almost non-existent. Yes, I still have those "senior moments", but they are few and far between.

I wrote several pieces, mostly in essay form regarding my struggles with acceptance of the diagnosis of dementia; mainly because I simply did not want to believe it. I watched my mother slip away into dementia the last 4 years of her life, visiting her almost weekly and watching her waste away into a world that I could not reach her in. It wasn't always bad. She told me amazing things about herself, not recognizing me as her son. In fact, for the last two years of her life she always referred to me as "John, from the bank". She asked me about her investments and if I was taking care of the house, etc. She talked about me with John quite often. Wondering why I had stopped visiting. It tore at my heart, but I told her "Bob" was coming by every week, but that she was usually sleeping and he didn't want to disturb her.

I will never forget her 85th birthday. I arranged a room for the party and several of my brothers and their families came to visit. She was having a lot of fun with it; posing for pictures, passing out hugs, etc. when Kim noticed she was starting to pull at her hair. That was one of the warning signs that she was confused and on the verge of panic. She motioned me over and whispered in my ear, "John, who are all these people?" I smiled and told her they were my family members and that they had come by to help me celebrate her birthday since the boys couldn't make it in. It put a huge smile on her face and enjoyed the rest of the party.

In this portion of my book, I will share my thoughts on aging, Alzheimer's and the twilight years of our lives. Some of them were written when I believed I was dealing with Alzheimer's; the symptoms were very similar, so I believe my observations could be of help to those dealing with the disease, either themselves or with loved ones.

I would especially like to dedicate this portion of my writings to Mike Moyers and Christine Ohl Robbins. They both have spouses with Alzheimer's and both have been tremendously supportive of me as I struggled through. I know that some of what I shared helped them both, as well as other friends of my through Facebook that had family members with dementia.

I hope it will be of value to someone who reads it.

Sincerely,
r m ullrich

Meeting Mom

March 9, 2008

Kim and Jackie, my step-daughter, met my mother for the first time today. Mom will probably not remember it, and if she does, she was convinced they were both my daughters. The ladies took an inordinate amount of pleasure in that, totally at my expense. At one point; mom smacked me and told me to stop picking on them! She then proceeded to tell Kim she could kick me out of the room if she wanted to so that "the girls could talk".

Whether or not my mother remembers them isn't the point. I was able to tell her that I had finally found the love of my life and that she made me very happy; happy like dad had made her. She was happy for me, so I know she understand that part of the conversation.

When it was time to go, she struggled to her feet to walk us to the door. She only got about 5 feet from the bed and I had to help her back over to lie down. She wasn't upset by the experience and proceeded to give both Kim and Jackie a big hug and a kiss on the cheek and told them they could come visit any time; and they didn't need to bring "John" along either.

If she makes it through to summer, we now have a picnic to plan for her. She will be expecting fried chicken, mashed potatoes (like her mom made), corn on the cob and all the fixin's. It could very well be one strange picnic experience, but a damn good one no doubt.

Enjoy the moments in life that leave you breathless. They can be few and far between.

Darkness Falls

I fight to live in the now
While battered by the past
Losing track of time so fast
That I wonder where it's gone
I breathe in deep
Wait for the moment to come
When my mind can see
What is meant to be
So wanting to be free
Of distant memories
Still clinging to me
Trapped between these walls
Living day by day
Until darkness falls

April 29, 2012

STOLEN WORDS
~September 5, 2011~

Time slips slowly past my window pane
Soon nothing but the past will remain
Locked forever in the misty recesses of my mind
Long dark paths cluttered and undefined

I don't know when it all began
But I do remember when it became
The day I looked upon nature's beauty
And couldn't remember her name

How will I know what I need to say?
When the words I know are taken away

It would be much easier to go it alone
To reach the end unencumbered
Nothing to remember but one last detail
When I found my days were numbered

I had it all planned out you see
Down to the end of time for me
Then she came and changed my life
And from my hand she slipped the knife

She tells me that I have nothing to fear
That she will forever be at my side
Even when my mind is no longer clear
And I've lost even my foolish pride

How will I thank her for all she'll have done?
When I won't even know she's the only one

How will I know what I need to say?
When the words I know are taken away

Time slipping slowly past my window pane
Soon nothing but the past will remain
Locked forever in the misty recesses of my mind
Long dark paths cluttered and undefined

How will I know what I need to say?
If all my words are stolen away

~Written for the one that loves me most while
I still have the words to say it~

YESTERYEARS

Hello again old friend
I'm glad you've come
It whiles away the hours
Setting my spirit free
Sharing
Caring
Sparing the sorrow
Hour after hour
Today or tomorrow
Keeping me company
Memories of yesteryear
Always clear
With you here
Smiling back at me
Reminding me
Regaling me
Amusing me
Setting my spirit free
Laughing with you
Stories about me
Memories of yesteryear
Always clear
While you are here
Smiling back at me
Time slips away
I know you can't always stay
Keeping me company
I know you have to go
There's something I must do
Yet before you leave
Help me to believe
You will come back to see me
It sets my spirit free

A whispered adieu
More for me more then for you
As you quietly slip away

~

The mist slowly clears
Revealing my tears
In the eyes looking back at me
In my faded mirror
Memories of yesteryears

~

~ December 4, 2012

Words

Saying what you think
Isn't easy as it seems
When the words come out all wrong
Saying what you mean
With words so out of sync
Makes for a day quite long
I reach out to those I love
Wanting to share my thoughts
And the words come out all wrong
Words
Simple words
Sometimes gentle
Sometimes not
Words
Weave the story
Tell the tale
Share the memory
Words
Forgotten words
Missing words
Forever dancing in the dark
Words
Glimmers of hope
Shades of fears
Blurred through the tears
Saying what I think
Was easy of a time
When the words flowed smoothly
Saying what I mean
Was never easy as it seemed
I simply wasn't afraid
I fear not for my own fate

Nor destiny now defined
Death has never been my enemy…
I fear living in a world of shadows
Not knowing the meaning of my strife
Locked away in memories of someone else's life

~

September 15, 2012

Faded Memories

Faintest smile touches her lips
Trying so hard to simply resist
One last look back in time
When surrendering to love wasn't a crime
Fading memories are beginning to slip
One last chance to take this trip
Back to another place and time
When she still felt his love sublime

They say that time can change the past
Making memories fade at last
Until nothing quite remains the same
Struggling to even remember his name
Yet the love still burns deep inside
A truth you can never hide
He loved you hard and left you broken
Heart still aching from the words spoken

Light laughter from her now
She truly can't resist
One more look back in time
When surrendering her love wasn't a crime
Fading memories starting to slip
She can't resist this one more trip
Back to the place and time
When she still knew his love sublime

Wondering how it ever died
Wondering had she done enough
Believing that he loves her still
Hoping that he always will
No matter the life's path taken
His was a love that can't be shaken
There is no reason to doubt now

He pledged his love with a sacred vow

Heartfelt sigh escapes her lips
Blood flowing from her fingertips
One last look back in time
One last hill left to climb
Before her life can come to pass
Leaving her heart like broken glass
Needing to know he loves her still
Wanting to believe he always will

Rest your weary soul in his love
Wear it around your heart as a glove
Memories like those won't fade to past
Memories of joys meant to last
Nothing can take that from you
Knowing your heart was true
Doing everything you could have
Giving him everything you should have
There's nothing left to say or do
To prove your love was true
No matter the time that life has taken
Yours is a love to be never shaken
There's no need to doubt it now
You pledged your love with a sacred vow

One last smile touches her lips
Trying ever so hard to simply resist
That one last look back in time
When giving him her love was never a crime
One last chance to take the trip
Before the memories begin to slip
Back to a long lost place and time
When she knew love so sublime

When faced with the choice of living or loving; chose love.
Living is temporal; love can surpass the end of time.

Hi, My Name is Robert Ullrich....

When we introduce ourselves it is a simple greeting. With our name we enter into conversations: start a meeting, open up a sales presentation, make new acquaintances or simply identify ourselves. I've done it thousands of times; we all have throughout our lives. It is after all, the name we were given, or chose to use.

The diagnosis of Alzheimer's has changed the way I look at my name. It is a challenge in my daily life to remember who Robert Ullrich is.

I read an analogy by a writer with Alzheimer's that at the end of his day his memories are like file folders scattered around the floor, and he tries to put them back into the filing cabinet where they belong, in the proper order. What I didn't understand was that the filing of the memories is just one aspect of the process.

As we all know, some memories are more pleasant than others. There have been experiences that molded my character, my personal ethics, morality and personality. Some of those experiences are wonderful memories, while others are dark and painful, and through the years (either by chance or by conscious design), I have forgotten many of them. Psychologists refer to memory suppression, cognitive dissonance and dissociative identity disorders. I call it human nature, or to be perfectly honest, my human nature.

The aspect of Alzheimer's that has become the hardest for me to deal with is differentiating between a memory, and a character facet. What I mean is that because I did something at one time in my life it doesn't define who I am, but it did have an effect molding my personality. Kim reminds me every night that something that I did in 1989 doesn't make me WHO I was in 1989. If you understand that, then you understand what I am trying to convey here.

I don't just remember experiences from my past more clearly, I relive them; some in my dreams and others while I am awake, occasionally at work. While my short-term memory continues to deteriorate, such is not the case for my long-term. With those memories come emotions as though it were today. Some memories are fulfilling. Some memories I went to great lengths to erase from my consciousness. Regardless, they are back, and often with a vengeance. I find myself as angry or as happy as I was then without regard for my current surroundings. It can be quite unnerving, not only to me but to those around me.

The end of every day is a process now. I try and separate the experiences of my past from the reality of my present. We all change, at least to some degree, and for some like me, the changes are drastic and life-altering. The person I was in 1989 is not the person I was in 1959, 1969, 1979 or 2009, let alone the person I was in 2011 when I was diagnosed with early onset dementia. There are days that I "feel" like the person I was in the experience I am re-living, particularly when it is something that most people would construe as a negative experience. I say most people, because I don't define an experience as negative or positive, but merely as an experience that contributed to the man I came to be at the age of 57. So-called negative experiences can have extremely positive results in the shaping of one's character, morality or personality, even at the expense of someone else's feelings, character or morality.

I am not defined by what I did to others; I was shaped by it. They were affected by it, but I am not completely responsible for the end result; no matter how often they blame me for it; they share the responsibility. I am not defined by what was done to me. I was molded by it. What was done to me is a reflection of the character, morality and personality of the other person, and I personally do not believe they are responsible for my end result. I am. Kim takes the time every night to listen to me sort through the folders, answering my questions truthfully whether I like it or not. I tell her of a past experience where I believe I wronged someone, wrong being based on what I can only call the generally accepted moral norms of our society at large, she tells me something positive that I did for someone else. She does not judge me, or what I did in the past as others would. She doesn't call me a sinner or a criminal; or tell me what I did was evil. She doesn't assign blame or guilt; when others have so many times in my life. She helps me find the Robert that I am in the midst of the memories of the Robert that I was.

My psychologist has been waiting for me to get angry about the diagnosis of Alzheimer's for two years. I don't understand why. I have no idea of why I should be angry, or what I should be angry about.

My positive effects will remain positive; the negative impacts I have had on others cannot be undone, changed or forgotten, at least not by me.

So, I sit in my chair every evening before going to sleep, sorting through the events of the day that I can remember and the events of my past that I cannot forget while Kim listens quietly in the shadows. She gives me something to hold on to, something positive to end my day with. That is a gift no one can repay, least of all me.

Peace to those who seek it, love to those that need it, judgment to those that deserve it.

That is my prayer for the day.

Sunday, March 22, 2015

Sunday Morning

It was a warm Sunday morning. The first I could remember for months. Winter was starting to slip into spring, if not quite willingly as there was one last hurrah left in her icy winds yet to come. No matter, for it was a harbinger of spring that reminded me that change was coming.

I was spending time with my mother as I have so many times in the past. The last year has found me spending more time watching and listening as she rambles, waiting for that moment of recognition that has become far more fleeting. Waiting for that moment in time when her eyes focus and she smiles at me. Sometimes, she asks, "Now, who are you again?" but usually she simply smiles and tells me it's good to see me again.

We were out in the dining/common area that day near a bank of windows on the southeast corner. Mom was in her "Barcalounger" as I have come to call it, and I was sitting on a couch next to her telling her stories of our lives like I often do when she is not responsive, or simply sleeping. I let her sleep most times, even though the nurses say it won't hurt to wake her. I read to her, or tell her stories and that is good enough for both of us I think. Many times Kim comes along with me, but this time I had come alone. Don't get me wrong; mom really took to Kim when they first met. Even welcomed her to the family, and then told me I could go check on her things, but I digress…

I had been rambling along for about an hour or so and was talking about summers in Des Moines when we were children. I had just mentioned Grandpa Henry when mom whispered softly "He's been gone for a long time". I stopped and looked at her. The eyes were bright and she was looking right at me. "Yes, he has been", I responded, half expecting her to simply go back to rocking and humming as she had been for the last two hours, but she didn't.

"I miss him" she went on, "and I miss Ron, too." I remember the smile that crossed her face then. It was a good thing to see. I told her I missed him, too, assuming that she either knew who I was, or was sure she knew me.

The next hour will be forever burned into my memories. We spoke about many things, some funny, some sad. We talked about her boys, all of them, so I knew then that she didn't know whom I was, but that doesn't bother me at all anymore. I talked about me as easily as I talked about the rest of my brothers. I even secured an answer to the question "Who is your favorite son?" I wasn't surprised by her answer, and believe me, she as adamant about it. I tried to suggest a couple other options and she didn't waver. As to which one was her favorite? Well, I can tell you this much, it wasn't me! (Although, I was happy to hear that she thought I was strong enough to deal with whatever came my way). As far as which one holds that title, and will hold it forever, I don't know if I will ever share that information… but she did ask me how they were all doing, one by one. I kept it light and upbeat, assuring her that they were all doing fine.

For the first time ever, she talked to me about dying. She said she was worried about how her boys would handle it. She said that some would do better than others, but she was still worried about leaving them behind. She made me swear to her that I would take care of them, look after them, so I swore it. I assured her that she would live on in their hearts and minds and in the hearts and minds of her grandchildren for decades to come. I truly believe that we carry a part of those we love on with us after they are gone. A bit of his or her spirit, or soul, or essence, whatever you may chose to call it. That seemed to ease her mind, and we continued on.

She grew quieter as the time passed, I think she was getting tired, but she never lost focus. She spoke in clear complete sentences for the first time in months. She didn't seem to have to strain to hear me, even though I spoke softly. At one point, I caught her looking at me out of the corner of her eye with what I can only describe as a wry grin on her face. I laughed and asked "What?"

"So, where are you going to plant me?" she asked.

I tried not to look shocked, but I think I failed because she laughed at me. "Well, I figured I would plant you next to Ron. I kind of thought that was what you wanted, and besides, the plot is already paid for." That got quite the chuckle out of her. I reminded her that she had a few things to say to Ron when she caught up to him and she agreed.

"That's right" she said, "I'm still pissed at him for leaving me!" and then had another good laugh. It was good to see her laughing again. Hell, it was good to see her again, period. I can't explain what I mean by that, but if you have ever watched a loved one slip away mentally, then there is no need to explain. Over the last year I have had some remarkable conversations with my mother. We have discussed elevators that can take you to where you used to live "Just like on Star Trek"… She also told Kim and me about the monkeys that played in the snow outside her window last winter. She popped me when I asked if they wore those little fezzes. "No" she said, "these are REAL monkeys, and you scare them away when you pulled back the curtain like that!"

After her hip-replacement surgery last summer, she told Kim and me stories about working for the Sheriff's department, the details of which forever changed the way I looked at her. It wasn't the first time she had told us about working for the sheriff, but this conversation was far more descriptive then the last ones had been! It never matters to me if the stories are true or not. I am, however pretty sure that elevator doesn't exist, and that the odds of capuchin monkeys frolicking in the fresh Iowa snows are greater than me winning the lottery…twice.

I stopped in to see mom again this week. The nurse tried to help me rouse her and we simply couldn't. I ended up sitting with her, holding her hand and talking to her like I have so many times before. I still don't mind. I sit there, waiting and watching for that look of recognition, of awareness. When she tells me she's afraid I tell her it's okay, that she's done enough, that it's okay to move on. This week, it didn't come, but who knows, maybe next time I will catch her looking at me out of the corner of her eye again…but if I don't, no matter…she truly has lived long enough.

April 11, 2009

Dust to Dust

I choose to live
With her by my side
Giving meaning to my day
Showing me a better way
Guiding me though this life
Keeping me from the strife
That will surely come my way
Not knowing what to say
I simply hold her close

Moment by moment you live
Your love is all you have to give
To show how much you care
Through life that's far from fair
It is what makes it worth living
The selflessly giving
Of all that you can share
Until your soul is laid bare
And you simply hold her close

Time is no longer on my side
There will never be enough for me and my bride
The years will pass ever so swiftly
Memories fading far too quickly
Ashes to ashes, dust to dust
No matter in which God I put my trust
I will lose my way in time
To a thief who commits no crime
And still she will hold me close…

August 9, 2012

Gone; but not forgotten

My father – Ron Ullrich
My mother – Jeri Ullrich
Laura Ullrich
Cindy – known to many by just that name
Diamond T. Black
Shelly
Julie Matthews – That Sassy little Leo Aussie from Armidale
The Lady Ahzmandia (Angel by name to those who loved her)

Will of Iron
August 26, 1989

Will of iron; hands of steel
With the touch of a velvet glove
Standing strong against the world
Unyielding in his hope and love

From rising sun to coming moon
He labored at his chosen trade
Many were the trials faced
Yet his heart seemed unafraid

His 6 sons stand before him now
Arrayed in their very best
Paying homage to this fallen man
To lay this warrior to his rest

Looking down upon their faces
A smile must light his eyes
Sending forth his unyielding love
On the wings of an angel it flies

"Fear not my sons though I am gone
For death is not the ending
I shall surely live on forever
Rest in this truth I am sending"

Will of iron; hands of steel
The touch of a velvet glove
Soaring aloft against the winds
Undying is his love

Always will he be near them
Though miles away it may seem
For this man will never die
As he lives on forever in their dreams

I had to fight to urge to edit this as I re-typed it. The only copy I have is from the Independence newspaper that my mother published it in. In the end, I added three words and took away two. The essence remains unchanged. I learned much from my father; much of which I didn't realize until I got clean in 1992. I can still see his face, and even more amazing to me; I can still hear the sound of his voice.

Sileo puteus meus Abbas

WHISPERED MEMORIES
February 19, 2009

Life's long journeys come to pass
Time to sleep is here at last
No more need to shed your tears
Hiding from the nighttime's fears
There's nothing left for you to do
Nothing left for you to say
No more reasons for you to pray
You did more than you should have
You did all that you could have
To make the world a better place
You left your mark in our hearts
Taught us all to do our parts
In life's sweet dance
We've taken the chance
And given it our best
Some better then the rest
But together we have learned
That the journey is what we've earned
No guarantee of the morrow

As to whether it brings happiness or sorrow
But it will arrive come what may
Because today can never stay
Neither can you or me
We are destined to be free
Of the bonds of flesh and bone
Never to be forgotten or alone
Slipping the winds of time
In whispered memories of our lives
~For my mother, Jeri (Geraldine Catherine Henrietta
Brabender Ullrich; in the twilight of her years ~

LAURA

Cold wind blowing today
Shivers run up my spine
Images dance in memories
Taking me back in time

Sweet smile on her lips
Devilish twinkle in her eye
Still so very young and free
How fast time flies

I see her holding my daughter
Whispering in her ear
Telling her she will learn to fly
That there is nothing there to fear

Strong of heart
Strong of will
Strong of mind
Stronger still

Gone from us so soon
I listen for her singing
Dancing on the moon
Another dawn she's bringing

Tears of sorrow on the morrow
Hearts torn asunder
Children left to wonder
Husband bereft of heart

A new day will dawn
In a not so distant time
When they will smile again
After time has healed their pain

In her name I will plant a tree
Knowing she would approve
Renewing again the circle of life
So that nature will bear her name

Cold wind blowing softly this day
Shivers run up my spine
Images dancing in my memories
Taking me back in time

Once again to see her smile
With a twinkle in her eye
Still so very young and free
Before the ravages of time

She held my daughter in her arms
Whispered words unknown
Words that lasted a lifetime
Still ringing in her ears

For my sister-in-law Laura, who, whether she knew it or not, convinced my daughter that nothing was beyond her grasp. Her words live on in my daughter Jessica, as surely as her love and memories live on in the lives of my brother Mark and her sons Paul and Jeff. She changed my daughter's world without knowing, even without trying. I will always love her for that, and honor the memory of her life by holding that in my heart.

4/12/2007

Dolphins Dance
(for Cindy)

Gazing out across the storm tossed sea,
her eye captures a fleeting movement.
White capped seas that toss and turn
waiting for a time that is heaven sent.
Dolphins dance in the broken surf
as seagulls announce the coming event.

Black hair flashing in the summer sun,
eyes filled with wonder at the sight.
The white-capped waves break over her feet
as the dolphins again take flight.

Long had she dreamed of the ocean's beauty,
hoping against hope to ever witness its glory.
Standing in awe of its majesty at last,
writing a last chapter to her story.

Through the day she runs and plays,
laughing and singing her song.
The dolphins dance in the broken surf,
as if nothing in the world could be wrong.

Night comes swiftly on the water
as the sun dips down into the sea.
Sitting now in the cooling sands;
knowing somehow she has been set free.

The morning sun finds the beaches bare.
The rolling waves the only sound.
Her footprints cover the sand for miles;
yet she is nowhere to be found.

The seagulls sit on rocks and watch;
the dolphins no longer taking flight.
The wind sighing in sorrow;
she was taken by Him in the night.

Forever we will remember you
whenever we hear their song.
Never will your smile be forgotten
while dolphins dance in the surf.

November 9, 2003
I know that Cindy lives on in her poetry; and in the hearts and of those that knew and loved her; like my dear friend Antonia did. I never got the chance to know Cindy very well. She always had a smile for me or a gentle comment or word of encouragement whenever we spoke. . It wasn't from my personal experiences that I was able to pen the above tribute to Cindy. I never knew about her desire to see the ocean and so many other things. Cindy passed away from cancer before she ever got to visit the seashore. I wrote this poem while listening to Antonia telling stories and sharing her love for Cindy. As my amica described her love for Cindy, I tried to capture the essence of it on paper. As she laughed and cried and whispered and wept I wrote the words you see above. When I finished, my amica was pleased with what I penned. That was enough for me, so I left it as written.

SHATTERED DREAMS

Silent screams for shattered dreams
Falling on deaf ears
Soundless rages against the night
Touch your deepest fears

Pain's sweet caress burns your soul
Fire scorches the ice
Shadows dance in the deep darkness
Now you must pay the price
Gazing down into the great abyss
Eyes of the lost peering back
Sounds of silence shatter your peace
Sunlight turns to black

All hope is gone in this shadowy realm
Desperation your only friend
Tortured souls share their agony with you
While you try to make amends
Reaching out to capture the wind
Flailing as you fall
Rocky crags rise to meet you
No one hears your call

Silent screams for shattered dreams
Falling on deaf ears
Soundless rages against the night
Touch your deepest fears

Through the thundering silence
Her voice caresses your skin
Words flow through your broken mind
Absolving you of your sin
Cool waters flood over your heart

Salvation now yours to take
At last your purpose is made clear to you
As you yield to the Lady of the Lake

Standing strong against the world
A warrior poet on the wall
Watching the demons battle for his soul
As he listens for her call

August 7, 2005

I wrote this for my friend Diamond at a time when he was living in peace after decades of fighting for survival on the mean streets of Chicago. This isn't one of my cheeriest pieces by far, but it is very much a story of triumph. When I came to know D, he had found his true love and surrendered his mind, body and soul to the one he called affectionately "HH".

It's been almost two years since they were taken from this world so quickly and violently that all that is left are our collective personal memories of them.

Kim, Jackie and I were in Chicago to visit them when everything went so terribly awry, and we never did get to enjoy that BBQ with them and their loved ones.

This is also another tribute to the memory of my mom, and her constant encouragement to share my writings with others.

Reckless Love

For Shelly
April 21, 2006

I see you sitting there
With that longing in your eyes
To feel the wind in your hair
To chase them clouds across the skies
I know it can't be easy
To sit there when you used to fly
I can almost feel my own heart break
When you light me up with that smile

Don't you hold back now girl
'Cause we both know the night is cold
Love with reckless abandon child
Love like you always rode

So many people wandering through life
Worrying about this and that
Thinking about the way it could have been
And missing the purr of a cat
I see you sitting there in that chair
That sweetest smile on your face
Living, loving and laughing so fair
Knowing you can still win the race

Don't you hold back now girl
Because we both know the night is cold
Love with reckless abandon child
Love like you always rode

Many a life has crossed my path
So many have come and gone
When I look down into your eyes

> I know I been blessed by this one
> I don't always thank Him
> Hell, I sometimes curse His name
> But when I think of your sweet kiss
> I smile and thank Him again
>
> Don't you hold back now girl
> Because we both know the night is cold
> Love with reckless abandon child
> Love like you always rode

Happy Birthday to that little sweetie who will ride the winds of time forever!

Thank you Shelly, for making me smile

Footnote: 4/20/2010

Shelly passed away in 2009. She never fully recovered from the injuries she sustained after being crushed under her horse in a fall back in 2005.

She loved that horse, and she loved to ride even more. In the years that passed from the time she fell, until the time she passed on, her life was filled with love and experiences beyond her wildest imaginations; thanks in no small part to Keith Urban, Kid Rock, Danni Leigh and some wonderful friends she made in the music industry.

She also found her true love and married before her time on this planet was complete. One of her greatest accomplishments was simply standing on her own at the altar to say her vows.

Shelly was an inspiration to many, myself included, as to how we should embrace the day. I will never forget her north Texas twang and the way her smile lit up the world.

I came across this piece I wrote for her on her birthday back in '06 and decided to share it. I hope it makes you smile a bit.

A Scorpio's Goodbye

Whatever the reason
Whatever the need
Now comes the season
When my heart will bleed
Never again to hear her voice
While forever left to rue the choice
That kept me from her side
To curse my endless pride
That cost her ever so much
When all she wanted was my touch

~

She never asked for anything
Turned my winters into spring
Made me laugh and made me cry
Now I'll wonder why she had to die
I know the reason in my mind
But reason fails me from time to time
And I rage against the gods
When they put my soul at odds
One last time I will say goodbye
And once again their wills defy

~

I will raise my voice in sorrow
For the loss I face upon the morrow
Morning left without the sun
For nighttime has truly begun
Always in my heart of hearts
Whenever the painful music starts
I will think of her and smile
Remembering a heart that knew no guile

They say it is appointed unto man
His way in this world alone to plan
Blessed was the day I found her
Among all the futures that there were
Karma brought us together
Many were the storms to weather
Destined never to share a touch
Perhaps the loss wouldn't be so much
What could have been…
What might have been…

So I will lift my voice on high
And sing a song unto the sky
The blessing of her unselfish love
Gone it seems to the heavens above
Taken from this world so young
So many songs left unsung…

Whatever the reason
Whatever the need
Now comes the season
When my heart will bleed

Never ending whispers of love
Captured at last in a mourning dove…

VESTIGES

Silence flows into silence
Listening in the still of the night
Faint whisper of imaginations
Memories dance in the distant shadows
Calling out your name
It will never be the same
No matter how long
The image still strong
Long after the night is gone
You could have…
You should have…
Now it's too late
No longer will I wait
In the misty recesses of my mind
Waiting and wondering
Why you never said goodbye…

Robert - March 7, 2011 - it is a difficult thing to lose a friend; especially one that loves you dearly. (I started writing this one in October of 2008. I finally found the right words.) Rest in peace Julie…

The testament to her love for me was her happiness when Kim entered my life. There are few people in this world that can truly do that. Julie did that for me. She encouraged me to pursue my life with Kim, and to never consider her love for me a detriment to my happiness. She wanted what was best for me. Julie died soon after Kim and I were married; taken from this world slowly and painfully. The last letter I received from her was about how her closest friends got together and took her on a two week cruise. They even arranged for her doctor to go with them in the event of a health crisis while at sea. She told me they were among the greatest two weeks of her life. Those are true friends.

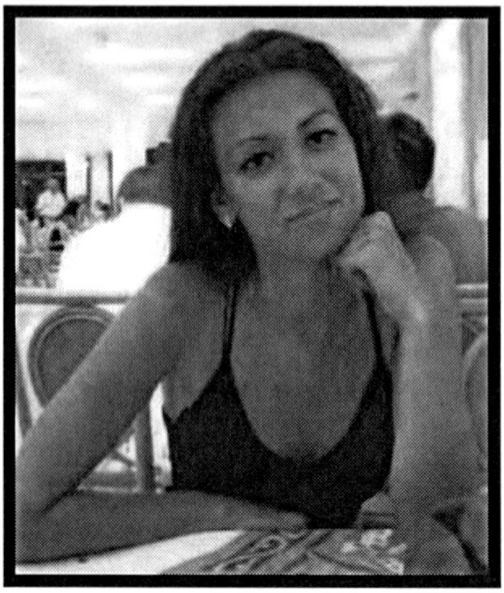

The Lady of the Lake

She was everything to him
The reason for the sun
She was everything to him
With her had life begun
She was everything to him
The reason for it all
She was everything to him
Without her, darkness falls

He was a lost and lonely man
Wandering the streets alone
Watching her from afar
Waiting for the chance to atone
Life lived without the taste of love
Burdened with a heart of stone
Wanting but to catch her eye
Knowing her smile would lift him on high

She was everything to him
The reason for the sun
She was everything to him
With her had life begun
She was everything to him
The reason for it all
She was everything to him
Without her, darkness falls

For 20 years he kept his peace
Watching over her in the night
Living life on darkness edge
Doing what he knew was right

The years stretched out before him
Keeping his dreams to himself
Embracing his fate and place in life
Watching over the one that would be his wife

For five short years he lived the truth
It was for her he was meant to be
Chosen in time to stand by her side
From chains of darkness free
That was when his life began
Born forever anew in love
No longer cursed to walk alone
Rescued by an angel from above

She was everything to him
The reason for the sun
She was everything to him
With her had life begun
She was everything to him

The reason for it all
She was everything to him
Without her, darkness falls

Faithful in death as he was in life
Avenging her loss with fire from above
Never stopping to count the cost
No reason to live in a world without love
They are together, have no fear
In eternity they wander together
The warrior poet and his Dragon Queen
Dancing forever on the edge of the abyss

She was everything to him
The reason for the sun
She was everything to him
With her had life begun

> She was everything to him
> The reason for it all
> She was everything to him
> Without her, darkness falls

For the Lady Ahzmandia and her Diamond ~ gone but not forgotten, not by a long way.

June 18, 2009

Those of you that know me know that I shared a love for the Lady and her Diamond that was not easy to define. We came from different worlds, but shared so much. They never judged me for who I was, or what I had done in life and neither did I judge them.

They accepted me as they accepted so many others, freely. They changed the lives of some so drastically that they barely survived the loss.

HH, as she was affectionately known to many, was my closest confidant and as a psychologist, one who helped me to accept myself and gave me the opportunity to help two young ladies that were battered and abused by life to find a safe place in this world with me where they could talk about anything and everything.

It's been about a year since the world moved on without them. I lost not only them; I lost the little dragon princesses, too. Lady A was the connection for us, the conduit between worlds as it were. I miss them. I miss them every day.

I wanted to put in words the essence of what Lady A meant to her Diamond. I don't know if I have captured that or not, but I tried.

Truth is Truth

I hear her knocking at the door…
Winter's on the move again
Slipping ever so deceptively closer
Enticing me with dreams of wintery beauty
Fresh fallen snows in pastoral settings
Precious little creatures frolicking about…
Winter turns my thoughts back in time
She does it every year
Yes, I look forward to the coming New Year
And she is bracketed by my favorite seasons
Autumn, when the colors ignite the forests
One last blaze of glory before the darkness settles
Spring, when new life blossoms on the barren land
Renewing my hope in an ever changing world
For now, however, the proximity of winter chills me
One last icy winter, this one will be
That reason alone gives me pause to reflect
Many and varied are the paths I have traveled
I have dined with the sinners and sung with the saints
Both have given me joy in their own way
Neither in the end, better than the other or so it would seem
For I have learned much from both after all
Don't ask me which has taught me more
Or better the way to walk in this world
But I will tell you this…
It wasn't from the pulpit I learned a great thing
It was from a man who was born of the streets
Raised in poverty and violence
Forsaken by society for the choices he made
From the mouth of a self-proclaimed thug
Came the words that tempered my soul

"Truth is truth"
It was his hand that passed out presents at the holidays
To children in pain in a world with little hope
It was this man that protected the innocent
By any religious standard he was condemned
He held no truck with the hypocrites of faith
I don't defend the choices he made
Neither do I condemn them
It wasn't my life he was living
Winter is coming…
She's just up the street watching
Waiting for her time
I will miss her someday, that much is true
But for now I will take my walks down memory lane with her
Reminiscing over paths taken, choices made
Loved ones long gone, friends old and new
And I will rejoice in the truth again
Truth is truth.

~

Robert~PS2K~November 22, 2009

BEFORE MY TIME

Living long enough
Has always been my desire
Not to live forever
Nor until the end of time
Rather living long enough
That I would be too old
To die before my time
Too old to die too young
Looking back I see it's true
That time has passed for me
I have seen my children grow
And my children's children, too
Lived long enough to know true love
Long enough to know real regret
Long enough to understand
That I have lived long enough
And that I am truly now
Too old to die too young
Memories abound yet to be created
As I travel the blessing way
One more day or a thousand thousands
Will not change what has been made
Nor alter the fact that truth is truth
And living long enough
Is simply all I ever wanted
And more than I deserved

~

July 7, 2013~ as always, I remain a work in progress with no end in sight.

It never ceases to make me smile when the haughty fall from grace. It's a bit ironic in and of itself, since many find me to be a bit arrogant, or so I have been told. Not to my face, mind you. I chuckle when I hear it because I would have to agree. My ex seemed to take particular offense when I said that some people are intrinsically worth more to this world then others. She hit me with the classic "all men are created equal in the eyes of God" tidbit. I don't necessarily concur with that thought either, but it isn't really important what I believe on that matter. The point I made was simple, and I will pose it to you as well. If you can convince me that Adolph Hitler was as good for mankind as say, Gandhi, or Jesus the Nazarene, then I will gladly concede that point to you. It won't change the way I see things, but I am willing to admit when someone makes a good point.

Nothing gives me more pleasure than watching one who thinks they are above the law, or untouchable be brought to bay. Politician, preacher, cleric of any flavor for that matter, chairman of the board, cop or criminal…

FOR BILLIE

I wonder where you'd be today
If not for that fateful spring day
When beneath the river's waters
You quietly slipped away
Alone in the darkness
No one to guide you
She tried to find you
She loves you to this day
As do I my long lost friend
We never got to say good bye
Over the years I have tried
Sitting by your side
Wiling away the hours
As the sun slowly fades
I would drive by the fields
Where I learned to ride
Where I learned to drive
Where I loved to work
Riding shotgun on a tractor
Fear and fun both a factor
As we turned the earth
Or harvested another crop
No one would believe
How much I loved you
I never knew why
Nor have I ever tried
To understand or explain
The hole that remains
Deep within my heart
I haven't visited in 3 years now
Life has taken me away
I left a flower that couldn't stay

As I tried one last time to have my say
But the tears still got in the way
Knowing I will see you again one day
And then I can say hello my friend
No longer to lament your untimely end
Until that day I will wonder
And time to time I will smile
At the memory of one particular day
Where you swore me to secrecy
A vow I have kept for over 40 years hence
I gave you my word
You gave me yours
You took my secret to the grave
I will take yours with me
Until we meet again my long lost friend

~

Robert U ~ 2/28/2013 ~ because I still remember

Contentment

Fiery touch of the dragon's breath
Washing over me as I lay here
Caressing my soul with her fire
Making all my thoughts so clear
Wrapping my arms around her
Feeling the passion in her breast
How the lion's heart beats for me
Deep within the dragon's chest
Two have become one in love
The dragon and lion joined together
No longer fearing the coming day
Any storm in his arms she will weather
Always watching over her heart
Never letting the lion run free
Safely now in the scorpion's grasp
There is no need to diligent be
And the two become one in love
The dragon and lion joined together
No longer fearing the coming day
His love for her any storm will weather

~

Sighing softly in my soul
Now a woman that makes me whole
Has come into my world
And watched my wings unfurl
The touch of dragon's breath
The beating of the lion's heart
There is no more fear of death
Smiling softly at the coming night
Holding her gently to my side
Watching the shadows run and hide
Knowing now the only reason

I wandered alone for such a season
Fiery touch of the dragon's breath
Washing over me as I lay here
Caressing my soul with her fire
Making all my thoughts so clear

~ July 30, 2007~

El Gusto es Mio

She makes my world a better place
with every smile that caresses her face…
She gives me peace in a world of strife
I will never be able to fully explain
The depths of love that she shares
But I will try
There has been enough sorrow
There is always enough pain to fill the morrow
So sacrifice in love
That which you cannot afford
Give of yourself until it hurts
Let that be the pain that remains
~ July 5, 2009.

HOME

I want to take her home
Back to the sea
Set her free again
Unfetter her soul
Unbind her spirit
Set her free
To be
What I know she can
What I have seen
Free to dance
Free to sing
Free to bring
Joy and laughter to my world
I want to take her there
By the water's edge
Warm southern breeze
Caressing her skin
Dolphins dancing in the surf
Full moon o'er the dunes
Dancing
Singing
Filling my world with laughter
Bringing life to me
Back by the sea
I pray to take her home
This I ask of thee
Father of my soul
This one last thing
Happiness to bring
To the one that loves me most.
2/5/2013

Memories, Observations and Lessons learned from a year in Montana (and the journey there and back again)

1. 2000 miles is a long drive.
2. Its longer when you have two dogs and a cat, with said cat howling in your ear for the first hour of every day on the road.
3. Its better to drive less and take longer to get there.
4. Montana is a lot like West Texas, with bigger mountains, way more snow and fewer pickup trucks.
5. The Rocky Mountains are majestic, magnificent, breathtaking and beautiful.
6. The Missouri River is the longest river in North America.
7. I still don't like driving in the snow; that will never change.
8. Elk are huge.
9. Bighorn sheep hang off the side of a cliff like a sparrow on a branch.
10. You have to really pay attention if you are ever going to see a Bighorn whilst traveling from Missoula to Great Falls.
11. There is nothing quite like family.
12. Family isn't always, or only about genetics.
13. I really like working in a wood shop.
14. There is a reason they call it Big Sky Country…and it is quite accurate.
15. The people in Montana are right neighborly as a rule.
16. Rattlesnakes are very polite.
17. Magpies, not so much.
18. 60,000 Canadian geese taking off from a field at the same time blocks out the sun.

19. Golden eagles are quite large, and for the record, still my favorite raptor.
20. Red-tailed hawks are everywhere.
21. If a pigeon flies into your warehouse through an open walk door, you can open every overhead door in the building and it still won't fly out on its own accord.
22. If a prairie falcon flies into your warehouse, just open one door and get out of its way.
23. F-15 Eagles are still my favorite fighter jet. No offense to the next generation of aviators.
24. It is kind of cool having a badge and handcuffs at work.
25. When someone you love passes away, they never leave you. I knew this already, but it was nice to have it reinforced.
26. A spiritual man is far more important to the world then all the religious leaders combined.
27. Good intentions are sometimes enough, no matter the outcome.
28. You cannot make someone truly happy; it's their choice whether or not to be so.
29. Having said that, there are some people that will make you happy simply by being themselves.
30. Pronghorns are amazingly fast.
31. There is a tremendous amount of energy at an old buffalo jump.
32. Prairie dogs are quite curious.
33. Banx will never catch Cheyenne in a dog race.
34. Kim will climb over two fences to pet a horse, although usually it was only one –electrified at that.
35. Going to Canada by accident can happen. For the record, I wasn't driving.
36. Canadian border agents are much friendlier then the US border agents.
37. Every day of my life is better simply because of my wife.
38. 7-year olds do not understand the concept of distance, but they have a pretty good handle on Skype.
39. I really can live without television for a year, but not without my DVD's.
40. Table saws are dangerous.
41. I miss the end of my pinky from time to time.

42. After cutting off the end of my right pinky finger, after having broken it in high school and the flesh ripped off the bone in 1974, it is officially NOT my lucky finger.
43. The wind rarely stops in Montana…
44. Time does cure all, if you want it to.
45. Holding on to the past eliminates your ability to participate in the present to any degree of satisfaction.
46. Some people may always be in your heart, but they won't be a part of your life.
47. Nothing that happens to you is worth having regrets about, as long as you learned from it.
48. One very important reminder was that some people will always mistake kindness for weakness.
49. I am never happier than when I am with Kim, no matter the circumstances or situation I find myself in.
50. I will end my list with this final thought: If I had it all to do again; the move to Montana that is: knowing what I know now looking back with the clarity of hindsight: I would do it all over again just to be where I am today, right here, right now with the one that loves me most.

Through the Tears

She came to me with tears in her eyes
Afraid she hadn't done enough for him
Wanting so much to ease his pain
Wanting so much for the joy to remain
Memories of long gone days of happiness
Mixed with the memories being made today
Together they wandered through the years
Through the tears
Avoiding the fears
Not looking at the inevitable
Embracing what they could
Avoiding what they should
Father and daughter in a dance of love
While the snow fell from above
Gently wafting to the frozen earth
Muffling the sounds of the passing years
Through their tears
Avoiding the fears
Full moon shedding her light down on them
Lighting up their smiles
For just a little while
Easing all the pain
Letting the happiness shine through the years
Through the tears
Without any fears
Of a tomorrow yet to come
When through the veil forever will come
Knocking gently on the door
Uniting them again forevermore
Father and daughter in a dance of love
While the snow falls gently from above

Gently wafting to the frozen earth
Reminding them of the sounds of years long past
When through the tears
They faced their fears
And embraced each other one last time
Under the watchful eye
Of the eagle who fell from the sky

~

For my wife and the man that raised her as his own. Thank you for making my life better, simply by seeing the love between you.

October 17, 2009

ONE

~

New day dawning bright
I can feel the sigh of the night
As the sun warms the air
And I see her standing there
Arms reaching out to me
Knowing that my heart is free
Whispers dancing in the mist
Of timeless love that does exist
Within her boundless soul
The caress that makes me whole

~

Seasons come and seasons go
Love and trust will grow
Between the two of us
Building on the trust
While a world that stands waiting
Anticipating
Debating
Hating
Berating
Desecrating
That which they don't understand
Unable to demand
That I obey their command
And kneel to the fallen gods
With whom I am at odds
For the lives they took
And the world they shook
To my very core
Wanting always more

New day dawning bright
I can feel the sigh of the night
As the sun warms the air
And I see her standing there
Arms reaching out to me
Knowing that my heart is free
Whispers dancing in the mist
Of timeless love that does exist
Within her boundless soul
The caress that makes me whole

Lives changed for all time
Hers and mine now intertwine
One path
One future
One life
One love
One desire
One fire
One hope
One moment
One kiss
Till that day
When the gods I must pay
And give her back to them

January 1, 2008 ~

    I wrote this piece soon after Kim had moved in with me, and it was like she was coming home. As 2010 unfolds before us, I am preparing to move again. This time, I am the one that is going home, and I am taking her with me. It is just a matter of time until we make our way to the Texas gulf coast. I have long since given up trying to understand why I have been blessed so much in my life. I can honestly say that I didn't do anything to deserve it, far from it to be frank. No matter, I accept the blessings and will simply give thanks every day for the love in my life, and to the one that saved me from myself, and made my life worth living. I wouldn't change a thing in my past, for to do so would alter forever the path of my life, and I would not be here…right here…right now…this moment in time; one moment, captured forever in a lifetime of moments. The past is a memory, the future but an illusion. All we have is now.